THE ARTIST AS DIVINE SYMBOL

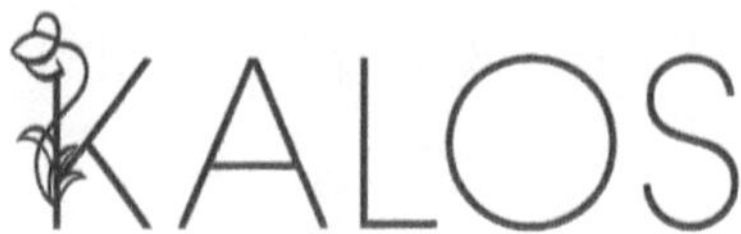

The word *kalos* (καλός) means beautiful. It is the call of the good; that which arouses interest, desire: "I am here." Beauty brings the appetite to rest at the same time as it wakens the mind from its daily slumber, calling us to look afresh at that which is before our very eyes. It makes virgins of us all, and of everything—there, before us, lies something that we never noticed before. Beauty consists in *integritas sive perfectio* (integrity and perfection) and *claritas* (brightness/clarity). It is the reason why we rise and why we sleep—that great night of dependence, one that reveals the borrowed existence of all things, if, that is, there is to be a thing at all, or if there is to be a person at all. Here lies the ground of all science, of philosophy, and of all theology, indeed, of our each and every day.

This series will seek to provide intelligent-yet-accessible volumes that have the innocence of beauty and of true adventure, and in so doing remind us all again of that which we took for granted, most of all thought itself.

SERIES EDITORS:

Conor Cunningham, Eric Austin Lee, and Christopher Ben Simpson

The Artist as Divine Symbol

Chesterton's Theological Aesthetic

Adam Edward Carnehl

CASCADE *Books* · Eugene, Oregon

THE ARTIST AS DIVINE SYMBOL
Chesterton's Theological Aesthetic

Kalos series

Cascade Books
An Imprint of Wipf and Stock Publishers
199 W. 8th Ave., Suite 3
Eugene, OR 97401

www.wipfandstock.com

PAPERBACK ISBN: 978-1-6667-6307-2
HARDCOVER ISBN: 978-1-6667-6308-9
EBOOK ISBN: 978-1-6667-6309-6

Cataloguing-in-Publication data:

Names: Carnehl, Adam Edward [author].

Title: The artist as divine symbol : Chesterton's theological aesthetic / by Adam Edward Carnehl.

Description: Eugene, OR: Cascade Books, 2023 | Series: Kalos | Includes bibliographical references and index.

Identifiers: ISBN 978-1-6667-6307-2 (paperback) | ISBN 978-1-6667-6308-9 (hardcover) | ISBN 978-1-6667-6309-6 (ebook)

Subjects: LCSH: Chesterton, G. K. (Gilbert Keith), 1874–1936. | Christianity and the arts. | Aesthetics—Religious aspects—Christianity. | Ruskin, John, 1819–1900. | Pater, Walter, 1839–1894. | Wilde, Oscar, 1854–1900.

Classification: BR115.A8 C37 2023 (print) | BR115.A8 (ebook)

10/05/23

For Lisa

A Poet a Painter a Musician an Architect : the Man

Or Woman who is not one of these is not a Christian

You must leave Fathers & Mothers & Houses &
Lands if they stand in the way of Art

—FROM WILLIAM BLAKE'S *LAOCOÖN*

The primary imagination I hold to be the living power and prime
agent of all human perception, and as a repetition in the finite
mind of the eternal act of creation in the infinite I AM.

—SAMUEL TAYLOR COLERIDGE, *BIOGRAPHIA LITERARIA*,
CHAPTER THIRTEEN

Contents

Preface

Chesterton writes in the final essay of *Heretics*, "Religious and philosophical beliefs are, indeed, as dangerous as fire, and nothing can take from them that beauty of danger. But there is only one way of really guarding ourselves against the excessive danger of them, and that is to be steeped in philosophy and soaked in religion."[1] I first read these lines as a high school student at a Lutheran camp in Michigan, sitting in a room called "The Ark," which was covered in murals painted by my father. I remember sitting in a little plastic chair and reading this line again and again, savoring it, and also knowing, somehow, that after reading Chesterton my life would be changed forever. A year or two before this my father had given me a copy of *Christian History* with a prominent article on Chesterton that noted his influence on C. S. Lewis. I have since lost this copy of the magazine, but I remember the large, black-and-white photo of the man and my feeling of fascination with him. After reading the essays of *Heretics* and *Orthodoxy*, that portrait of Chesterton kept creeping back into my mind. His large cape and stern gaze seemed to emphasize the fact that he was up to something much more dangerous and romantic than the contemporary world could handle. Chesterton had realized fully, at the dawn of the last century, that "The dogmas we really hold are far more fantastic, and, perhaps, far more beautiful than we think."[2] Reading Chesterton was surprising and challenging, and already at that age, I knew I wanted to read him for the rest of my life.

This century might very well be the century that finally takes Chesterton not simply as a witty, minor writer who merits a footnote or short article in an encyclopedia of English literature, but as one of the most original Christian thinkers at the turn of the twentieth century. Indeed,

---

1. Chesterton, *Heretics*, 298–99.
2. *Heretics*, 303–4.

in the last several decades, more and more serious theologians have begun to write on Chesterton, identifying his insights and contributions to the field of theology.[3] In a discipline that is often accused of academic in-speak, of engaging in obtuse arguments over minute, scholastic problems while ignoring the concrete problems of the present age, Chesterton emerges as a kind of unusual, entertaining maverick who always had much to say about every conceivable vice and folly of modernity. Capable of arguing with the sharpest minds while humorously dismantling the greatest attacks on his beloved church, the journalist could quote from memory important lines from Shakespeare, Pope, Browning, Dickens, Swinburne, and hosts of other authors and poets while explaining difficult theological problems, offering insightful, fresh conclusions in typically humorous and often very brilliant ways. In his incredible, personal absorption and integration of English and French painting, poetry, drama, literature, criticism, fairy tales, folk stories, classic legends, and world mythology, he is an astonishingly broad, startlingly modern, refreshingly interdisciplinary thinker himself. And in all of his oeuvre, from the early essays just before 1900 to his *Autobiography* of 1936, Chesterton gives us a thoroughly Christian, thoroughly exciting vision of the Truth.

The impetus then for writing this book comes from my time as a theology graduate student in Scotland. Between 2016 and 2017 I was at the University of Glasgow studying under two scholars known for their great work in the field of theology and the arts, George Pattison and David Jasper. Back then I had originally set my sights on the Russian existentialist Nicolas Berdyaev, wishing to explore his esoteric Christianity, specifically his original work on creativity and theurgy. However, the influence of Chesterton on my own thought and development was too strong to ignore. I do not remember fully how the shift from Berdyaev to Chesterton happened (perhaps it was something as unexpected as my noticing that they share the same birth year, 1874, though Chesterton died a decade before Berdyaev), but I began reading Chesterton in earnest, especially early Chesterton, and then especially early obscure and overlooked Chesterton. Then, after noticing how frequently he was in conversation with others, I began widely reading things from his opponents, friends, and

---

3. See, for example, Fagerberg, *The Size of Chesterton's Catholicism*, as well as Milbank, *Chesterton and Tolkien as Theologians.* Also see Reyburn, *Seeing Things as They Are.* Fagerberg is a liturgical theologian and Milbank is a philosophical theologian who works at the intersection of literature and theology; Reyburn is a lecturer in visual arts who understands Chesterton's religious ideas well.

most importantly, his nineteenth-century influences. I still had in mind some project that generally fitted within theological aesthetics, but I was not quite sure how everything would coalesce. Yet, after reading certain critics whom Chesterton seemed to continually pick fights with—specifically John Ruskin, Walter Pater, and Oscar Wilde—and then stumbling across some of Chesterton's unjustly neglected yet highly original works of *art* criticism, I realized that, far from most contemporary depictions of Chesterton as primarily a polemicist and apologist, he was, from his early days, an acute art critic.

This book is the result of these personal and academic discoveries, which I believe first begun in my teenage years and were brought out most fully while researching at Glasgow. My hope for this book is not to introduce another generation to Chesterton; if I do this, very well and good, but it would be incidental to my purpose. Many fine writers and speakers have already introduced Chesterton to our age.[4] In very many ways I am indebted to these people, for it is due to their labors of re-publishing Chesterton's works, passing along Chesterton's ideas, establishing Chestertonian clubs and reading groups, and presenting his ideas to ordinary Christians via magazines, books, blogs, and podcasts that I came to discover him and begin reading him in the first place. Yet, neither do I hope to give an overview of Chesterton's career or an evaluation of his multifaceted thought. Again, I can think of several fine books and articles that do exactly this. Rather, I hope to bring out an aspect of Chesterton's early work that has been overlooked: his insightful criticism of painters and art critics toward the beginning of his career. In doing this, I also want to re-introduce contemporary readers, especially Christian students and scholars who might not read Ruskin, Pater, or Wilde regularly, to these brilliant aesthetic thinkers.

Chesterton's criticism of the artists of his day is both enlightening and entertaining, and it is in conversation with those three critics in particular—Ruskin, Pater, and Wilde—that Chesterton begins to develop some of his most intriguing theological aesthetic insights. When I was a student at Glasgow, I realized that it was therefore necessary to elucidate the heart of their own aesthetic theories and then to connect them to the late-Victorian religious situation. I came to realize that where Ruskin needs a firm aesthetic and philosophical foundation for his own

---

4. There are even graphic novels and children's books about G. K. Chesterton, which I believe would humble him more than any movement or school named after him.

faith, both Pater and Wilde ever seek to disentangle beauty from previous foundations, in order to elevate beauty to its own foundation, and therefore, to a new kind of religion. But all three critics struggled with the exact relation between God and aesthetics, Christianity and beauty, and none of them reached the firm conclusions that classical, Christian theology (of the kind that Chesterton espoused) achieved in relating these things together.

Chesterton has been unjustly neglected in most academic studies of aesthetics during the *fin-de-siècle*, and it is my hope that this current study can demonstrate his importance. It is true that the "Fleet Street journalist" has not been as influential as Ruskin, Pater, or Wilde to the development of English literature or English aesthetics, but this is precisely the reason why I believe his aesthetic thought deserves to be more closely examined now. Chesterton is a helpful figure because he comes from a time in early-twentieth-century Great Britain when there was widespread fascination among poets, artists, and theologians with Catholicism and mysticism, theosophy and magic. Yet, he rises above this time. There is something about Chesterton that is perennially interesting, original, prophetic. I believe that he is in his most brilliant moods in the writings before the First World War. This is the decade that gave us his magnificent works *Heretics* and *Orthodoxy*, and it is also the period when he was closest to people such as Yeats and other Symbolist authors. It was, furthermore, the time in which he wrote his two books on individual painters. In the twenty-first century it is becoming more and more apparent that Chesterton *is* one of the most important Christian writers from the beginning of the last century, and personally, I believe he is certainly the most interesting and entertaining. Prolific in every way, there are still many surprises to find in his novels, stories, essays, journals, treatises, and letters, and, as the decades pass, more and more new readers will be engaging with his work. I hope that my book can be a small contribution to this ongoing, exciting conversation all sorts of people are having about GKC.

Morris County, New Jersey
Feast of St. Valentine, 2023
Adam Edward Carnehl

Acknowledgments

This book grew out of a dissertation I originally wrote for my theology degree at the University of Glasgow in Scotland. I am thankful for my two supervisors, the Reverend Professors George Pattison and David Jasper, who are not only outstanding scholars but also model churchmen and mentors. I have them to thank for their continual support, even for me now as this project has evolved. Professor Pattison was an immense help in understanding the genius of John Ruskin and the broad field of theological aesthetics. Professor Jasper's encyclopedic knowledge of Victorian literature was and still is invaluable to me. He was always ready to read my material and offer helpful suggestions. Our many discussions on the nineteenth century's critical spirit also opened my eyes to the importance of Chesterton's early work.

My congregation while in Glasgow, St Columba's Lutheran Church in East Kilbride, was ever supportive of my research and gave my wife and me much encouragement while we lived far away from family and friends. The congregation that I serve now, Good Shepherd Lutheran Church in Randolph, New Jersey, is also highly supportive of my academic interests. Since I came to them in December of 2021, they've never stopped helping me with prayers and funds to buy more books. I am grateful to God for giving me such warm and wonderful congregations while doing this research and writing.

It is fitting that I originally submitted my dissertation on the feast day of St Finbar of Cork. A first edition of the *Autobiography* of Chesterton was given to me by Brother Finbar of Pluscarden Abbey in Moray, Scotland during the writing of the thesis on which this book is based. I have him and all the brothers to thank for their kindness in showing me such hospitality while staying at the abbey to pray, meditate, and reflect on this research.

I am deeply appreciative to all the folks at Wipf and Stock, the Cascade imprint, and the editors of the KALOS series for all their encouragement, help, and support. I have only hearty thanks to give my editor, Dr. Robin Parry. I am also beyond grateful to my Doktorvater, Conor Cunningham, for his help, advice, and encouragement as this book came to fruition. Likewise, I am very grateful to Alison Milbank for guidance she offered in an email exchange.

Naturally, I have my family and friends to thank from my heart. While a teenager, two mentors of mine introduced me to G. K. Chesterton and discussed him with me. These men, my lifelong friends, are R. J. Moeller and Daniel Hase. They are still changing young people's lives, especially as they now raise their own children. My parents, Jeffrey and Janet Carnehl, raised me to admire beauty and to exercise my creativity. They have also continuously supported my academic and artistic pursuits. My aunt, Charlene Kaiser, was kind enough to obtain for my library the complete Library Works of John Ruskin, a meticulously edited, profusely illustrated thirty-nine-volume set that is unbelievably rare and difficult to obtain these days. I cannot thank her enough for these gorgeous books that have aided me so much in my research.

My two young children, Gwen and Theodore, were sweet and kind whenever their dad had to go into the basement or over to his study to do more writing, and I know that as they grow up, they'll always see the mark of the Divine Creator in the true, the good, and the beautiful. I thank God for them. And finally, I must thank my wife, Lisa Grace, for all she does for me, our family, and the church. For over a decade she has been my bride, my companion, my friend, my muse.

Abbreviations

MP I / MP II   *Modern Painters*, volumes 1 and 2

Introduction

AT THE TURN OF the twentieth century, a colorful and original critic formulated his own Christian symbolist approach to some of the religious and aesthetic *aporias* of the preceding Victorian era. The critic is a frequently underestimated one, Gilbert Keith Chesterton, and the narrative is a thoroughly well-known one: the "honest doubt" of the Victorian Age.[1] Rather than looking at Chesterton's Christian apologetic as outlined in his more well-known texts, in this book I focus upon his less famous and less discussed art critical works. My argument is that in these early works Chesterton establishes an original, theological aesthetic that recovers a Catholic and mystical understanding of God's presence from the post-Romantic skepticism and aesthetic fragmentation of the age. Chesterton's original contribution is his vision of artistic creativity, which is a true reflection of humanity's divine center, where the "image of God" has been manifested and restored by the incarnate God, Jesus Christ.

In making these claims for Chesterton, there are several challenges that come to the fore. As an autodidact and as a popular author he is notoriously difficult to characterize. He stands outside of mainstream schools of thought and conventional scholarship on religious philosophy from the time period. Today he is remembered almost chiefly as a Roman Catholic apologist, a quick wit, and a popular candidate for sainthood.[2] Yet, as I will outline below, Chesterton, in his writings on art, brilliantly pulls together important Victorian approaches to art and Christianity in Great Britain at the time of the *fin de siècle*. These approaches are primarily represented by John Ruskin's "theoria" and the response by Walter Pater and Oscar Wilde in their call of "art for art's sake," an aesthetic philosophy that attempted to preserve some sense of the sacred through the

---

1. See the classic study: Miller, *The Disappearance of God.*
2. Parker, "A Most Unlikely Saint."

elevation of the experience of beauty. Ruskin, Pater, and Wilde struggled to find a place for religious meaning in the face of new, critical schools of thought originating from thinkers as diverse as David Strauss and Charles Darwin, Ernest Renan and Herbert Spencer.

Therefore, in this book I will establish how Chesterton followed the trajectory of art critics like Ruskin, Pater, and Wilde, and then aesthetically re-validated the mystical and sacramental claims of Christianity.[3] I make no overbold claims for Chesterton; he did not initiate a movement in the arts nor is he well-known for a particular philosophical work on aesthetics. He was not educated at either Oxford or Cambridge, and he was not a trained philosopher or theologian. He typically does not make an appearance in conventional studies of English philosophy or aesthetics. However, Chesterton was an enormously creative critic, poet, and artist who was a friend (or often a friendly critic) of a staggering number of the key English artists, writers, and critics of the *fin de siècle*. In his freedom from the restraints of the academy, Chesterton embarked upon a theological-aesthetic project in the first decade of his journalistic career, following his own inclinations and faith, and in this unique work he demonstrates a penetrating insight into the nineteenth-century struggle between faith and doubt.

Before outlining Chesterton's connections to the other three writers and before more fully exploring the nature of his contribution to religion and aesthetics, it would be helpful to establish the religious and aesthetic backgrounds to the Victorian age. Thus, in the remaining sections of this introduction, I will give an overview of the religious and aesthetic contexts that shaped the literature, art, and criticism at the end of the nineteenth century in Great Britain. Following this, I will introduce the critical and artistic projects of Chesterton, relating his thought to these Victorian movements that preceded his career.

---

3. At a time when others, such as Friedrich Von Hügel, Evelyn Underhill, and many other Roman Catholics and Anglo-Catholics were undertaking a similar project through their studies of mysticism through the devotional literature through the centuries. See Underhil, *Mysticism*. Also see Von Hügel, *The Mystical Element of Religion as Studied in Saint Catherine of Genoa and Her Friends*. Yet, Chesterton's view of mysticism is unique among his contemporaries. As I will discuss in chapter 3, he validated mysticism as a corporate and "democratic" experience of the primordial mystery that underlies all things, that is, the eternal truths God has stamped on creation.

The Shape of Religion at the End of the Century in Britain

J. Hillis Miller's classic, 1963 work, *The Disappearance of God*, recounts the breakdown of traditional religious conceptions of God and the Bible in the post-Romantic era. Miller's work is concerned with five Victorian authors: De Quincey, Browning, Brontë, Arnold, and Hopkins, and how their quests "might be defined as so many heroic attempts to recover immanence in a world of transcendence."[4] That is, these and other writers sought, in their creative work, to discover a God that was close and recognizable, despite the general feeling that God had become far more distant in such a skeptical age. Miller's thesis is that these five writers take the disappearance of God as "a starting place and presupposition," and that with such a beginning they then seek unity and organizing principles through their creative work.[5] Their writings, then, are indicative of wider social and cultural approaches to Christianity during this period. Miller's work is important for establishing the way artists and writers thought about their complicated relation to God during the era and even sought a reconstruction of their belief.

Miller notes that a "fragmentation" happened in the modern era—a fragmentation of "man, God, nature, and language," one that has come about by the increasing social, material, and technological transformations, from Protestantism to urbanization.[6] In an important passage, Miller notes, "When the old system of symbols binding man to God has finally evaporated man finds himself alone and in spiritual poverty. Modern times begin when man confronts his isolation, his separation from everything outside himself."[7] Hence Miller is just one of many critics of nineteenth-century British culture who sees this era as one marked both by grave doubts in traditional forms of religion and intense longing after creative, new understandings of religion.

Miller is far from being alone in his interpretations. E. S. Shaffer reaches similar conclusions. We read in Shaffer's classic study, *"Kubla Khan" and the Fall of Jerusalem* (1975),

> As dogma was psychologized, the personal experience of religious feeling became increasingly important; and this personal experience had to centre on Christ. Yet historical and

4. Miller, *The Disappearance of God*, 15.

5. Miller, *The Disappearance of God*, 15.

6. Miller, *The Disappearance of God*, 3–6.

7. Miller, *The Disappearance of God*, 7.

> psychological rationalism made the primary matter of Christianity—the Crucifixion and Resurrection—repugnant to the young men of the 1790s. Their nascent mythological understanding told them inescapably that the vision of Christ was the fundamental experience of Christianity; and that their age was incapable of it. All the writers of this period flutter on this pin. . . . Strauss finally carried this tendency to its extreme point in his fully mythological history of Christ's life.[8]

Even if the historicity of certain scriptural events was hard to swallow for these critics and freethinkers (these "young men" of the last decade of the eighteenth century), the issue was almost rendered moot anyway as adherence to dogma gave way to emphasis upon religious feeling. The "mythological understanding" of the stories of the church and the emphasis or focus on a subjective "religion of the heart" was to continue throughout critical circles during the Victorian era.[9]

In her work, Shaffer mentions the significance of theologians such as David Strauss (1808–74), a towering theological voice of the century, who offered a modern, critical reading of the Christian Scriptures and of their chief figure, Jesus Christ. At this time, Strauss and others, such as Matthew Arnold in Great Britain and Ernest Renan in France, were acknowledging that the Christian texts do indeed carry a profound message, yet it is a message that, like mythology, may have timeless, symbolical significance with little or no actual rooted historicity. The essence of the Bible's symbolic message—its powerful *ideas*—transcended time and setting. In his *Das Leben Jesu* (1836) (first translated into English by George Eliot as *The Life of Jesus Critically Examined*), Strauss writes, "Though I may conceive that the divine spirit in a state of renunciation and abasement becomes the human, and that the human nature in its return into and above itself becomes the divine; this does not help me to conceive more easily, how the divine and human natures can have constituted the distinct and yet united portions of an historical person."[10] For Strauss it is the *idea* of Christ as God united with humanity that contains immense power, whether or not the historical person was exactly as the New Testament writers described him. Strauss thought the idea of Christ was the important, transhistorical truth and that other details of his life or impact were time-bound, legendary additions. He explains, "It

8. Shaffer, *"Kubla Khan,"* 59.

9. For more on this, see the fascinating study: Van Horn, *Within My Heart*.

10. Strauss, *The Life of Jesus Critically Examined*, 779.

is Humanity that dies, rises, and ascends to heaven, for from the negation of its phenomenal life there ever proceeds a higher spiritual life; from the suppression of its mortality as a personal, national, and terrestrial spirit, arises its union with the infinite spirit of the heavens."[11] Strauss does not have in mind a supernatural process, but a worldly one. "By faith in this Christ, especially in his death and resurrection, man is justified before God; that is, by the kindling within him of the idea of Humanity, the individual man participates in the divinely human life of the species."[12]

This conception of Jesus Christ, shared by the emerging critical theologians during the century, sent shockwaves throughout the West. Shaffer provides further elucidation of the century's change of theological thinking when she writes, "The more the theology of the age came to stress Christ as the link between man and a distant God, or, like Schleiermacher, Christ himself as man, the more He too became cut off from God."[13] With the idea that God is now a distant force, not a personal and immanent person, new anxieties and pressures arose in the Victorian mind. The result was a re-orientation of the Christian religion from something otherworldly to something worldly; its documents and figures began to be regarded as myths and legends, though of the highest, most important sort. "Christianity, then, is Hellenism developed and ordered, the evolved summary of all mythological revelations from the beginning of experienced time by which the race comes to understand the moral truths of its own nature";[14] Shaffer demonstrates that as a result of this mythologizing of the Christian Bible, post-Romantic thinkers began to see Christ not as a divine savior, mediator, or intercessor, but simply as a very great—perhaps the greatest—poet.[15]

The French historian Ernest Renan also impacted European conceptions of Jesus Christ, though his approach to Christ in the Gospels was of a different sort than Strauss. His work, The *Life of Jesus* (1863), represents the same appreciative yet highly critical spirit moving through the century. Renan writes, "That the Gospels are in part legendary is evident, since they are full of miracles and of the supernatural; but legends

11. Strauss, *The Life of Jesus Critically Examined*, 780.

12. Strauss, *The Life of Jesus Critically Examined*, 780.

13. Shaffer, *"Kubla Khan,"* 61.

14. Shaffer, *"Kubla Khan,"* 187.

15. Shaffer, *"Kubla Khan,"* 223. This was a perspective that was not lost on Wilde, who described Christ as poet and artist during the decadence of the *fin de siècle*.

have not all the same value."[16] This implies that the documents of the New Testament are of a higher value than other legends. Because of their imaginative power and the unique influence of the man, Jesus Christ, the Gospels are of inestimable worth—but they are still legends, to be interpreted mythologically. "Jesus is the highest of these pillars which show to man whence he comes, and whither he ought to tend. In him was condensed all that is good and elevated in our nature. He was not sinless. . . ."[17] Renan goes on, casting doubt upon the traditional narratives and symbols of the Christian faith yet praising the man Jesus as an ideal individual to emulate and respect. Again, like Strauss's arguments, Renan's work caused considerable shockwaves in educated circles during the nineteenth century.

I will also situate the English poet, critic, and essayist Matthew Arnold here, following Strauss and Renan, for the impact his views on Christ and Christianity made on the Victorian mind. Arnold's work must be read in the context of his poem, "Dover Beach" (1867), where he illustrates the situation of religious faith in his century:

> The Sea of Faith
> Was once, too, at the full, and round earth's shore
> Lay like the folds of a bright girdle furled.
> But now I only hear
> Its melancholy, long, withdrawing roar,
> Retreating, to the breath
> Of the night-wind, down the vast edges drear
> And naked shingles of the world.[18]

For Arnold a return to the traditions of this "Sea of Faith" was unthinkable. Though Christianity once, like the sea, lay "round the earth's shore," now it is withdrawing, retreating, receding, not because fewer people were converting to Christianity,[19] but because it was increasingly difficult for contemporary philosophers and *literati* to accept the tenets of traditional

---

16. Renan, *The Life of Jesus*, 6.

17. Renan, *The Life of Jesus*, 227.

18. Arnold, "Dover Beach," 210–12.

19. Timothy Larsen has helpfully pointed out that many high-profile atheist or agnostic writers actually converted to Christianity, and that, overall, in the nineteenth century, reconversion amongst lapsed academics, lecturers, and writers was fairly widespread. Larsen's observations are not as convincing when we look at the critical philosophers and high-profile academics during the age, but his nuanced study does need to be considered. See Larsen, *Crisis of Doubt.*

Christianity. Arnold's significant work *Literature & Dogma* (1873) seeks to recover some sense of ethical truth in the wake of widespread doubt. Arnold's conclusion, that the Bible is a guide to ethical conduct, that "conduct makes up ¾ of life,"[20] means that the eschatological, sacramental, mystical, and liturgical elements from Christianity are dispensable, and that what remains is a kernel of moral imperatives. Arnold still thinks Christianity and the Bible important enough, in some way, to devote much of his energies to defending their value, but he implies that their value for the contemporary, nineteenth-century world is drastically different than past ages recognized.

Therefore, traditional notions of God and Christian theology were receding during the post-Romantic age, but the reality of religious sensibilities was ever present. In a contemporary introduction to the literature and religion of the period, Mark Knight and Emma Mason write, "Christianity in particular interrogated and reconstructed itself over and over . . . stirred by new approaches to Scripture, doctrine, and the structure of the Church and its community."[21] The authors further conclude, "Religion was not just another aspect of the nineteenth century: it found its way into every area of life, from family to politics, sport to work, church architecture to philanthropy."[22] Religion also found its way in the symbolic and artistic imagination in the Victorian era. Indeed, in Ruskin's writings, even during his famous period of doubt,[23] we see biblical allusions pepper

20. Arnold, *Literature & Dogma*, 20.

21. Knight and Mason, *Nineteenth-Century Religion and Literature*, 7.

22. Knight and Mason, *Nineteenth-Century Religion and Literature*, 9.

23. For more on this, see Hilton, *John Ruskin*, 254. Much ink has been spilled on the nature of Ruskin's period of religious disturbance or doubt. Ruskin himself identifies a particular moment in 1858 when he experienced a "crisis in the whole turn of my thoughts" and became a "conclusively *un*-converted man" in Letter 76 in *Fors Clavigera* (April 1877); see Cook and Wedderburn, *Works of John Ruskin* (Library Edition), 29:89. The story Ruskin tells is that he wandered into a Waldensian chapel in Turin and heard a sermon that so angered him he became disgusted with much of his Evangelical upbringing. Yet, in the following decades, Ruskin did not become an outright atheist, but his Christian faith underwent a deep change. For an interesting interpretation of Ruskin's lifelong Christian sensibilities (and even orthodoxy), see Nichols, *All Great Art Is Praise*, 22–30. A view by Ruskin scholar Dinah Birch is also helpful here: "[Ruskin] never lost his faith in the Bible as a repository of human and divine wisdom, as others had lost or were losing such faith; indeed he grew yet closer to the Bible during those years. The change in his position was not that he came to value the Bible less, but that he grew to revere mythology more." See Birch, *Ruskin's Myths*, 48 (note that Nichols quotes this interpretation in *All Great Art Is Praise*, 29). Also, immensely helpful in this regard are the careful conclusions reached by Michael

most critical and literary works. Pater and Wilde, in their call for "art for art's sake," likewise fill their works with theological and biblical language. Therefore, in late Victorian Great Britain, art and the imagination were impacted by the critical religious sensibilities of the time and also by the critical and philosophical currents originating from the continent. The next section will give a brief overview of the major philosophical aesthetic ideas that German philosophers introduced in the Romantic age. Along with the critical spirit of the age which was giving new interpretations of the core tenets and texts of Christianity, these philosophical aesthetic ideas—especially those of Kant, Schelling, and Hegel—would exert considerable influence on notions of art, beauty, and imagination in nineteenth-century Great Britain.

German Philosophical Influences on Victorian Aesthetics

Through the writings of Coleridge and Carlyle, and, later in the century, Walter Pater, the German philosophical aesthetic of G. W. F. Hegel and his followers "was brought fully into the mainstream as a challenge to the spirit of the age in Victorian England."[24] German idealism had a decisive effect on British philosophy, and though Ruskin decried almost anything that smelled of German culture or philosophy, even he, like our other critics, was influenced by the spirit of Hegelianism in the air of Britain during the century.[25] These philosophers generally held an exceedingly high view of art, seeing such human pursuits of architecture, sculpture, painting, music, and poetry as means of understanding the movement of the Spirit and the uncovering the power of ideas in human history. Yet in their estimation, art held a similar intuitive and revelatory power to religion, even serving as organized religion's (i.e., Christianity's) replacement

---

Wheeler in *Ruskin's God*. In the closing part of the introduction, Wheeler writes, "Susceptible as Ruskin's beliefs were to his own sharpened critical awareness, what never left him, and what proved to be least susceptible to the application of new critical tools by the scientists and biblical scholars of the day, was a belief in divine wisdom and the God of peace; and what came closest to resolving the conflict between the desire of his physical eye and the claims of his spiritual eye was a nexus of symbols and traditions associated with wisdom, the temple, and Solomon—types of the Holy Spirit, the sanctified Christian soul and the Christ whose bequest to the world, and to Ruskin, was peace." From Wheeler, *Ruskin's God*, 26.

24. Simpson, *German Aesthetic and Literary Criticism*, 24.

25. See Collingwood, *Ruskin's Philosophy*, 15, 21. See also Birch, *Ruskin's Myths*, 48–50.

and truest expression. For these philosophers, art, like the Christian Scriptures, held immense power over the human imagination, culture, and society. This was a power that relied not upon time-bound, historical events but timeless experiences—the perpetual unveiling of Pure Spirit. Yet with these German philosophers, specifically Kant, we see a fragmentation of the original unity between art and religion, aesthetics and metaphysics, history and mythology, imagination and morality. In the wake of Kant, the forms of religion were further separated from dogmatic content and appreciated for their own aesthetic. Strauss, Renan, and the other critics of the century continued in their own way this process of fragmentation. At the conclusion to this section, I shall briefly take up Coleridge as the key British figure that disseminated the Germans' aesthetic ideas in Great Britain.[26]

The Aesthetics of Kant and German Idealism[27]

Immanuel Kant, the giant of the German Enlightenment, tackles the philosophical concept of the *Beautiful* in the "Critique of Aesthetic Judgment" portion in his major work, *The Critique of Judgment*, but does not deal with interpretations of specific artworks or individual artists. In Kant's attempt at conducting an empirical investigation of beauty he utilizes a concept called "subjective universality." Kant disagrees strongly with the notion that beauty is arbitrarily decided by societies and their tastes through time; instead, he holds that all individuals across societies universally experience beauty, and this simply must be observed as a general rule.[28] Therefore, something is beautiful not because it is considered so across time and especially not because it is either useful or expedient; something is beautiful because it simply *is*, regardless of the specific responses to beauty that individuals might have.[29] Kant writes, "There

26. In the following analyses I rely upon the collection of German philosophical texts collected and edited by David Simpson: *German Aesthetic and Literary Criticism*.

27. A critical engagement with other Germans that have notable aesthetic theories, such as Hamann, Jacobi, Herder, Schiller, Goethe, and Novalis, is beyond the scope of this study. My intention is to highlight the major contours of the aesthetic thought of those few German philosophers who significantly impacted Coleridge's thought, and therefore through him, the aesthetic notions of Ruskin, Pater, Wilde, and Chesterton. The most important three would be Kant, Schelling, and Hegel.

28. Simpson, *German Aesthetic and Literary Criticism*, 43.

29. Simpson, *German Aesthetic and Literary Criticism*, 38–39.

can, therefore, be no rule according to which any one is to be compelled to recognize anything as beautiful."[30] The beautiful simply is taken as a given, as an observable "subjective universality." This means the "beautiful" is therefore both detached from metaphysical or religious concepts, and devoid of ethical (utilitarian) import.

This is not to say that Kant thinks that beauty (or the sublime) leaves the individual unaffected. He actually observes that an experience of the sublime in nature—that which is awesome and overwhelming by its sheer grandeur—is closely linked, in some way, to a person's moral fiber. All of nature, for Kant, "should at least show a trace or give a hint that it contains in itself some ground or other for assuming a uniform accordance of its products with our wholly disinterested delight" and in that hint the human mind finds its "interest engaged" in a somewhat moral way.[31] Kant does not fully elaborate how one's moral nature is affected by the sublime or beautiful in nature, but he suggests that the experience of these delights in nature is best received by the moral individual: "One, then, who takes such an interest in the beautiful in nature can only do so in so far as he has previously set his interest deep in the foundations of the morally good."[32] Kant grants some relation between morality and the subjective reception of sublimity and beauty, but for the philosopher from Königsberg, it is simply observable that those who are interested in the morally good are more likely to enjoy nature's beauty, and when they do, they are more likely to be delighted.

What we see in Kant therefore is a propensity to connect moral feelings to experiences of the sublime, but without the possibility of an explanation in metaphysical or theological terms; it is simply an observed and experienced inference. Also to note in Kant is that God is neither the source nor goal of beauty. The beauty or sublimity of natural phenomena or human-made artefacts is experienced in the same way regardless of the existence of God. God may be a helpful *concept*, as he is in ethics for example, but his absence in Kant's aesthetic is significant.

F. W. J. Schelling (1775–1854) was a professor of philosophy at various German universities and was originally a disciple of Johann Gottlieb Fichte, until he went his own direction.[33] Schelling's aesthetics hold a

30. Simpson, *German Aesthetic and Literary Criticism*, 39–40.

31. Simpson, *German Aesthetic and Literary Criticism*, 59.

32. Simpson, *German Aesthetic and Literary Criticism*, 59.

33. Drabble, *The Oxford Companion to English Literature*, 872.

central role in his philosophy. "I am convinced that the highest act of reason, the one in which she encompasses all Ideas, is an aesthetic act. . . . The philosopher must possess just as much aesthetic power as the poet. . . . [T]he poetic act alone will outlive all the arts and sciences."[34] This is because, for Schelling, art is a *revelation*, an act that unveils the highest truths. He writes that "art is the sole and eternal revelation that exists and the miracle which, even if it had existed only once, must have persuaded us of the absolute reality of that highest principle."[35] Talking of art as "revelation" and "miracle" is far from Kant's measured words on why individuals have a common subjective conception of "the beautiful." Schelling asserts that philosophy and all of the sciences "were born and nurtured by poetry in the childhood of science," and for him, the time is coming when all subjects will return to that "ocean of poetry."[36] Because the artist's work functions as an outlet for pure Spirit, Schelling is able to write, "Absolute objectivity is given to art alone."[37] The goal of the artist must be to withdraw from nature, not to mimic it and therefore produce empty masks, but to "emulate this spirit of nature, which is at work in the core of things"; this emulation will enable the artist to raise herself or himself to the level of creative energy, where the universal, that is, the spirit in nature, is expressed in the creative work.[38] It is because the universal essence of all things is unveiled through art that Schelling is able to give the study of aesthetics top priority in his idealist philosophy.

In his *Aesthetics: Lectures on Fine Art* (1823–29), G. W. F. Hegel (1770–1831) turns his full attention to the fine arts and traces a philosophy of history through the artistic developments within cultures. Hegel's philosophy sought to overcome the duality of Kant's system by finding the spiritual unity of the Idea behind all things; each thesis and antithesis in the universe leads to a synthesis.[39] More than any of the previous German idealists, Hegel sees in the arts an expression of the Spirit becoming

---

34. From Schelling's introductory note to his *System of Transcendental Realism*, quoted in Simpson, *German Aesthetic and Literary Criticism*, 119.

35. Simpson, *German Aesthetic and Literary Criticism*, 123. For someone coming to Schelling for the first time after having read Coleridge's prose works, the German idealist would sound awfully familiar!

36. Simpson, *German Aesthetic and Literary Criticism*, 130.

37. Simpson, *German Aesthetic and Literary Criticism*, 130.

38. Simpson, *German Aesthetic and Literary Criticism*, 151. These words are originally from Schelling's *The Relation of the Plastic Arts to Nature*.

39. Drabble, *Oxford Companion to English Literature*, 448.

materialized in human society; for this purpose, the study of aesthetics is decidedly important in developing a philosophy of history, which is a foreign idea to Kant. Hegel is not interested in people's subjective reactions to art but rather in the broad effects that art has had on the universal human spirit through time.[40] For the philosopher, art is a revealer of ideas as a mode of the Spirit. It simply cannot exist "for its own sake." The philosopher writes, "But nevertheless the work of art, as a sensuous object, is not merely for sensuous apprehension; its standing is of such a kind that, though sensuous, it is essentially at the same time for spiritual apprehension; the spirit is meant to be affected by it and to find some satisfaction in it."[41]

Interestingly, Hegel makes a remark in his introduction to *Aesthetics: Lectures on Fine Art* about the beauty of Catholicism. In his discussion of the proper "topic" (i.e., the subject or model) for the artist, Hegel writes that generally a topic will be given to the artist necessarily from the outside in the form of a civic or religious commission. Hegel admits that an artist then weaves his or her own genius into the topic given from outside, but "the more detailed individualization is not his. For this purpose he needs his supply of images. . . . [The topic] always remains to him a material which is not in itself directly the substance of his own consciousness."[42] Thus an artist is constricted somewhat in that the subject is given to him or her from the outside, but each artist also weaves personal material into the creative interpretation of that subject. Hegel goes on to write, "It is therefore no help to him to adopt again, as that substance, so to say, past world-views, i.e. to propose to root himself firmly in one of these ways of looking at things, e.g. to turn Roman Catholic as in recent times many have done for art's sake in order to give stability to their mind and to give the character of something absolute to the specifically limited character of their artistic product in itself."[43] Intriguingly, Hegel points out (somewhat disparagingly) that many in his day had turned to Roman Catholicism as a stabilizing foundation or normative power that could give a deeper meaning to artistic production than would otherwise be possible. He admits the system that is the Roman Catholic Church thus

40. Simpson, *German Aesthetic and Literary Criticism*, 208, 211.

41. Simpson, *German Aesthetic and Literary Criticism*, 210.

42. Simpson, *German Aesthetic and Literary Criticism*, 228–29.

43. Simpson, *German Aesthetic and Literary Criticism*, 229.

has a kind of legitimizing effect on art products, giving otherwise limited things a rooted, spiritual substance.

German Aesthetics Translated into English Literature

Finally, I would like to briefly look at S. T. Coleridge (1772–1834) as a key translator of German idealist aesthetics and metaphysics, not only into the English language, but into the English sensibility, though he did this in his own highly idiosyncratic way. It was specifically Coleridge's reading of Schelling that impacted his ideas behind the poetic imagination, ideas that would prove to be highly influential on other English authors.[44] It is well beyond the scope of this study to interpret Coleridge so thoroughly as to present a comprehensive picture of his multi-faceted interpretation of Christian symbols, but some comments must be made here on Coleridge's theory of the *symbol*, and specifically the symbols of Christianity, since this symbolic theory underlies much of aesthetic thinking in the Victorian age. As Coleridge outlined, the core symbols of Christianity are the figures and events recorded in the Old and New Testaments: these are themselves "the living educts of the imagination," and are "harmonious in themselves, and consubstantial with the truths of which they are the conductors, . . . past and future are virtually contained in the present."[45] Owen Barfield explains this theory when he notes, "We cannot comprehend nature without first having grasped that the whole may be 'in' each part, besides being composed *of* all its parts. We cannot comprehend imagination, or revelation, in literature without first having grasped that that very fact provides the distinction between a symbol and a metaphor."[46] The symbol has a mediating influence, linking past to present and eternity; it does not reduce a figure or story to non-history. A symbol, to quote Coleridge, "is characterised . . . [a]bove all by the translucence of the eternal through and in the temporal. It always partakes of the reality which it renders intelligible."[47] In his important though meandering work *Biographia Literaria*, Coleridge writes in chapter 9, "An idea, in the highest sense of that word, cannot

44. Drabble, *Oxford Companion to English Literature*, 872.

45. Coleridge, "The Statesman's Manual," included in White, *Political Tracts*, 25.

46. Barfield, *What Coleridge Thought*, 157.

47. Coleridge, "The Statesman's Manual," included in White, *Political Tracts*, 25.

be conveyed but by a *symbol*,"[48] and later claims that the "best part of human language" is formed from symbols which are affixed to internal acts of the mind, "to processes and results of imagination."[49] Language and art are symbolic. The symbol conveys an idea that it simultaneously participates in. It is through Coleridge, therefore, that Schelling and the idealists' ruminations on the symbol enter the educated circles of England. With Coleridge, this teaching on the great power of the symbol can now expand and fill the void left by the modern, skeptical dismissal of Bible and the Christian sacraments.[50]

The German Philosophers and Victorian Art Criticism

The Victorian writers that I am analyzing in this study, Ruskin, Pater, and Wilde, were fundamentally influenced by these philosophical ideas. A comprehensive work on philosophical aesthetics by Paul Guyer helpfully situates Ruskin in the same camp as these German philosophers because they all shared the presupposition that beauty is linked to truth. Guyer writes in his *History of Modern Aesthetics* (2014) that in Ruskin's *Modern Painters* there is

> a theoretical dimension that aligned Ruskin squarely with the philosophical aesthetics that, as we have seen, dominated the first half of the nineteenth century, the aesthetics of truth. As already suggested, Ruskin's version of the aesthetics of truth would then produce a powerful reaction, in the first instance the movement known as aestheticism or "art for art's sake," which does not so much try to amplify Ruskin's theory as to undercut the need for aesthetic theory altogether, arguing that aesthetic experience is a domain of pleasure that needs no explanation or justification from other areas of human experience.[51]

Guyer sees Ruskin as a kind of mid-century continuation of Hegel's aesthetics of truth, in contrast to Kant's aesthetics of free play or Mill's

48. Coleridge, *Biographia Literaria*, 71. Italics are his.

49. Coleridge, *Biographia Literaria*, 172.

50. The sacraments being the means of participation between earthly and heavenly, material and spiritual.

51. Guyer, *A History of Modern Aesthetics*, 2:191. Also observe here that, importantly, Guyer notes how Ruskin's aesthetic theories created a powerful reaction: *aestheticism*, the call of "art for art's sake."

aesthetics of conviction/emotion.[52] Guyer then also notes, most helpfully, that the "art for art's sake" approach arises as a response to Ruskin's strongly truth-oriented aesthetic.

Interpreters and critics have noted that Ruskin had other Hegelian tendencies as well. For example, the philosopher R. G. Collingwood pointed out that the author of *Modern Painters* never read Hegel but was a Hegelian in his belief in the "unity and indivisibility of the spirit," in his habit of reaching synthetic conclusions through the contradiction of opposites, and in his interpretation of history as being composed of creative epochs that deserve to be admired rather than imitated.[53] During and immediately after his lifetime, philosophers were attempting to discover the philosophical influences on Ruskin. R. G. Collingwood wrote a short book on Ruskin's philosophy, which was first given as an address to the "Ruskin Centenary Conference" in 1919, and went into great detail about his thought's dialectic and synthetic qualities.[54]

Scholars have also long noted the influence Hegelianism had upon Pater and Wilde (and even, to a lesser extent, Chesterton).[55] Eric Warner and Graham Hough, in their excellent anthology of nineteenth-century British aesthetic writings, *Strangeness and Beauty* (1983), track Pater's intellectual development. They note that Pater gained his Hegelian notions from the influence of his Oxford mentor Benjamin Jowett and from his own reading of the German philosopher.[56] Throughout his essays in *The Renaissance*, Pater, "regards cultural evolution as a series of renascences or rebirths, and which connects the 'outbreak of spirit' in the Renaissance back through the High Middle Ages to ancient Greece, as well as forward

52. Guyer, *A History of Modern Aesthetics*, 2:86, 121.

53. Collingwood, *Ruskin's Philosophy*, 15, 21.

54. Collingwood, *Ruskin's Philosophy*, 43. Here Collingwood helpfully points out the five major features of Ruskin's philosophical thought, noting that Ruskin's ideas were intuited and not studied in philosophical tomes. The five features of Ruskin's philosophy are: 1. It is historical and dialectical—not mathematical. 2. It dismisses scholastic definitions. 3. It is super-imaginative. 4. It is widely synthetic. 5. It emphasizes the indivisibility and wholeness of the spirit.

55. See Lauer, *G. K. Chesterton: Philosopher without Portfolio*, 46–48. Lauer's exploration of both Hegel and Chesterton's interest in the "primacy of ideas" over mere matter is illuminating. Out of all the works written on Chesterton's thought, I find this to be the most stimulating. It's worth noting that Lauer was a specialist on the philosophies of Hegel and Husserl.

56. See Warner and Hough, *Strangeness and Beauty*, 1:5.

to the Romantic Revival of Pater's own century."[57] To elucidate this assertion, more recently, Pater scholar Giles Whiteley writes,

> The identification of means and ends is, once again, that Hegelian subject-object identity which Pater had made foundational to his aestheticism. In other words, Pater's Hegelianism demands that he "treat life in the spirit of art"; this is its own internal necessity. Because art is beautiful and because beauty is the sensible appearance of the Idea, so too life must be treated as art in that it too is an example of the Idea made sensible. . . . Life is then art, the Idea made sensible, and thus the very substance of Morality (namely Reason).[58]

Pater was highly conversant with idealist philosophy, carried aspects of Hegel's aesthetics into his own, and even helped to establish a culture of Hegelianism at Oxford in the latter half of the century.[59]

The German philosopher and his followers exerted a tremendous influence on British aesthetics in the nineteenth century. Thus, these three critics: Ruskin, Pater, and Wilde, continued the extended conversation on aesthetics and morality, truth, and religion that the German idealists and English Romantics had been having. Taking into account the "honest doubt" narrative of the century, which stemmed from the cultural feelings on the disappearance of God as well as the perceived obsolescence of religious faith, the writers I am analyzing here had a wide variety of critical voices, agnostic and Christian, German and British, which influenced their own aesthetics.

Connections to Chesterton

The influence of German idealism with all its aesthetic-moral "fragmentation," the "honest doubt" narrative of Victorianism, and the critical re-evaluation of Christianity now leads us to consider the response of G. K. Chesterton at the turn of the century. In this book I take Chesterton seriously as an aesthetic thinker who is able to make a contribution to the *fin-de-siècle* conversation about beauty's relation to truth, morality, and God. I will seek first to establish the context, the influences, and the

57. Warner and Hough, *Strangeness and Beauty*, 1:6.

58. Whiteley, *Aestheticism and the Philosophy of Death*, 43.

59. Whiteley, *Aestheticism and the Philosophy of Death*, 21. Also see Drabble, *Oxford Companion to English Literature*, 448: "Hegel enjoyed a vogue in philosophical circles in England, particularly at Oxford, in the 1880s and 1890s."

major Victorian positions before moving on to describe Chesterton's original aesthetic contribution. Over the past century of popular and scholarly reflection on Chesterton, most have overlooked his theological aesthetics and relegated his art criticism to a footnote on the beginnings of his journalistic career.

Chesterton's literary output is so vast that for this study I must be highly selective in the texts I use to demonstrate Chesterton's theological-aesthetic position. So, I will examine those art-critical works from the first decade or so of his career, 1899–1910. This was an astonishingly fruitful period, with Chesterton publishing some twenty-six books by my count and many hundreds of essays, poems, and book reviews. Out of all of these I focus on the only two books he wrote on individual artists: *G. F. Watts* (1904) and *William Blake* (1910). I have also selected early essays from various periodicals where Chesterton first developed a Christian, symbolist response to Ruskin, Pater, and Wilde.[60]

In a recent and thorough biography of Chesterton, the late Roman Catholic scholar Ian Ker mentions some of Chesterton's early aesthetic essays almost in passing, and Ker does not offer significant analysis.[61] Ker's point is biographical, and he merely proves that Chesterton was quite a young man when he began writing reviews of art books. William Oddie, in a work that is far more analytical of Chesterton's thought, is nevertheless noticeably vague regarding Chesterton's aesthetics. Oddie dedicates several pages to Chesterton's early aesthetic writings but reaches conclusions only regarding his "fluency of [his] style, [and] intellectual boldness" as well as his "perceptive and original critical writing."[62] Although Oddie's book is one of the most thorough analyses of Chesterton's intellectual development, he only notes the importance of these early pieces as representing the rudiments of Chesterton's later, mature ideas. In other words, Oddie uses these critical reviews to make comments about Chesterton's "intellectual range" rather than to develop a picture of how Chesterton was continuing the ongoing argument over aesthetics stretching from Kant through to Ruskin and the aesthetes.[63] In another work, the Roman Catholic writer Gary Wills develops a better picture of

60. Most of these essays are not found in currently published collections. Some were co-written with a friend, J. Hodder-Williams, while others were published anonymously or under the initials "G.K.C."

61. Ker, *G. K. Chesterton*, 39.

62. Oddie, *Chesterton and the Romance of Orthodoxy*, 175.

63. Oddie, *Chesterton and the Romance of Orthodoxy*, 175.

the aesthetic and philosophical portrait of Chesterton than the others. Wills writes, "He did not take the ordinary critic's approach, discussing schools, influence, etc. He approached art from the side of metaphysics, looking to the artifact's own mode of existence."[64] Wills's point is significant in noting this important characteristic; Chesterton himself cared little for academic accuracy or biographical detail; rather, he cared about the revelation of truth behind any given artist's creative work. Wills is echoed by Hegel scholar Quentin Lauer who has noted the similarities between Hegel and Chesterton, that both were preoccupied with the "primacy of ideas."[65] Lauer's project does not include any of Chesterton's art critical work, however, and he does not connect the journalist to any art movement of his day.

Two books that directly deal with Chesterton's art or art criticism are *The Art of G. K. Chesterton*, by Alzina Stone Dale (1985), and *The Christian Imagination: G. K. Chesterton on the Arts*, by Thomas C. Peters (2000). Dale includes a helpful index to every illustration Chesterton published in his lifetime, but her book is more of an introduction to Chesterton's life than it is an analysis of his aesthetic philosophy. Peters looks at Chesterton's "imagination" through the lens of his illustrations and fictional characters. His is a popular-level work intended as an introduction to Chesterton's optimistic outlook. In that, it is successful for pointing out the journalist's unique, imagistic perspective, but it is not concerned to develop an analysis of it.

In light of these recent biographies and (now standard) secondary works, we can say that few have ever regarded Chesterton as firstly or principally an art critic. Self-described simply as an "old journalist,"[66] it is because of his great variety of creative and critical work that opinions on him have varied so dramatically over the last hundred years. H. Marshall McLuhan writes that "it is no contradiction to say that Chesterton is primarily an intellectual poet."[67] Orwell considered him to be the "most outstanding proponent" of "Roman Catholic propaganda."[68] Auden writes,

---

64. Wills, *Chesterton*, 70.

65. Lauer, *G. K. Chesterton: Philosopher without Portfolio*, 47.

66. Chesterton, *Autobiography*, 183.

67. Conlon, *G. K. Chesterton: A Half Century of Views*, 10. This is one of the most valuable critical works on Chesterton as it gathers fifty years of opinions about Chesterton from various critics, novelists, poets, and other writers.

68. Conlon, *G. K. Chesterton: A Half Century of Views*, 102.

"By natural gift, Chesterton, was, I think, essentially a comic poet."[69] Gide esteemed his literary criticism, calling his *Dickens* and *Browning* "masterpieces of comprehension and psychological insight."[70] The late political historian Margaret Canovan regarded him as a "free floating intellectual outside all political parties" who can be helpfully interpreted as a "populist" thinker,[71] while the translator, priest, and fellow Catholic convert, Ronald Knox, labeled Chesterton "an artist in thought."[72]

Chesterton may, indeed, be interpreted in a variety of ways, from witty comic poet to Catholic apologist to radical populist, but it as an art critic or aesthetician that I wish to consider him in this project. Perhaps it is the observation of his friend Ronald Knox that comes closest to my argument. Chesterton approached truth in an *aesthetic* way. For him, all artistic productions were symbolic keys to higher truths, and all such higher truths could never be fully disclosed by language, but only symbolized by art. Chesterton arose onto the scene in about 1900, the same time that symbolists such as Huysmans, Maeterlinck, Yeats, and Symons were highly influential.[73] I believe it is helpful to understand Chesterton as a kind of (broadly) Catholic symbolist, and I will be developing this argument throughout the book.

However, for now, lest Chesterton's connections to the preceding Victorian age, and especially the aesthetics of Ruskin, Pater, and Wilde, be questioned, I will now present what I have found to be some of the journalist's earliest and most interesting interactions with their thought and work.

Chesterton, Ruskin, Pater, and Wilde

A recent secondary work on Chesterton makes the claim, "Chesterton was an astute and appreciative critic of Victorian culture, defending

---

69. Conlon, *G. K. Chesterton: A Half Century of Views*, 323.

70. Conlon, *G. K. Chesterton: A Reappraisal*, 411.

71. Canovan, *G. K. Chesterton: Radical Populist*, 9.

72. Conlon, *G. K. Chesterton: A Half Century of Views*, 46.

73. Joris-Karl Huysmans (1848–1907), French symbolist novelist also much admired by Wilde; Maurice Maeterlinck (1862–1949), Belgian symbolist playwright and essayist; W. B. Yeats (1865–1939), immensely influential Irish symbolist poet; Arthur Symons (1865–1945), English critic who is remembered today for introducing England to the French symbolists; see Drabble, *Oxford Companion to English Literature*, 488, 606, 1093, 957.

writers that Modernists routinely debunked and desecrated. Unlike some of his contemporaries, he was capable of seeing past the apparent obsolescence of art that others deemed unfashionable."[74] One of these figures whom modern art theorists did consider obsolete was John Ruskin. Chesterton began writing in June of 1895 an unsigned book review appeared in the English periodical *The Academy* concerning a new Ruskin reader that had been edited by W. G. Collingwood.[75] This book review was the first journalistic piece G. K. Chesterton published in his life.[76] In the short review Chesterton does not offer an exhaustive interpretation of Ruskin; he does, however, point out that Ruskin (who was at this time an elderly recluse) has been "pathetically" exploited by so many persons, the publisher notwithstanding, who give him a "hesitating, condescending, and qualified approval."[77] Furthermore, *The Ruskin Reader* only presents the most eloquent passages of early Ruskin, and so presents a modified, palatable Ruskin, presented without his most challenging teachings. Chesterton regrets that this man of high caliber and achievements, who gave his "fortune and life to the service of others," is so badly misrepresented in this particular selection.[78]

Just three months after Ruskin's death, Chesterton furnishes us with another estimation of the Victorian art critic. Before his review was published in *The Speaker*'s April 1900 issue, Chesterton had written a letter to his soon-to-be wife saying, "I have got a really important job in reviewing—The Life of Ruskin [*sic*] for the Speaker. As I have precisely 73 theories about Ruskin it will be brilliant and condensed."[79] Chesterton's review again deals with a book published in 1900 by W. G. Collingwood.[80] In the article Chesterton asserts that Ruskin "was the last of the prophets," because of his "courage to mount a pulpit above the head of his fellows." He goes on to write, "He rushed from one end of a city to another comparing ceilings. His limbs were weary, his clothes were torn, and in his eyes was that unfathomable joy of life which man will never

74. Beaumont and Ingleby, *G. K. Chesterton, London and Modernity*, 6.

75. W. G. Collingwood, ed., *The Ruskin Reader* (London: George Allen, 1895).

76. Ker, *G. K. Chesterton*, 39.

77. Chesterton (unsigned), "The Ruskin Reader," 523.

78. Chesterton (unsigned), "The Ruskin Reader," 523.

79. Letter quoted in Ker, *G. K. Chesterton*, 66.

80. See Collingwood, *The Life of John Ruskin*.

know again until once more he takes himself seriously. . . . But he made what he praised in the old Italian pictures—'an opening into eternity.'"[81]

In considering these two early book reviews, we see that even in his early twenties, Chesterton held a sympathetic stance toward Ruskin, esteemed him to be a Victorian prophet, and believed contemporary criticism had entirely missed Ruskin's main teachings. Yet, perhaps the most interesting aspect of Chesterton's relation to Ruskin is found in the letter to his wife; it shows that Chesterton was well-acquainted with Ruskin's work and had many hypotheses on such a very complex figure.

Furthermore, before 1914 Chesterton wrote several essays on Ruskin, which appeared in various periodicals. One of them, later reprinted (with slight alterations) in *Varied Types*,[82] was the article he had written years previously for *The Bookman*; another was a more substantial article from 1908 simply titled "John Ruskin," and later reprinted in *A Handful of Authors*.[83] In this paper Chesterton takes a look at Ruskin's career and acknowledges: "The main thing that Ruskin existed to preach was this: that life (in the vital sense of vitality) is not a thing of gasps and spasms, but a thing consecutive, interdependent, nay laborious. Life that is alive, he meant, is continuous. Life that is alive is even conventional."[84] There is a veiled critique of Pater, Wilde, and the aesthetes in this sentence. For in the "art for art's sake" point of view, life is a series of unconnected moments of pleasure, of "gasps" and "spasms" of beauty seeping into an otherwise dull world.[85] He goes on to muse on Ruskin's views of art and writes, "Art means diminution. If what you want is largeness, the universe as it is is large enough for anybody. Art exists solely in order to create a miniature universe, a working model of the universe, a toy universe which we can play with as a child plays with a toy theatre."[86] Here Chesterton confronts the reader with a paradox: art at once presents a

81. Chesterton ("G. K. C."), "Ruskin," 107–8.

82. Chesterton, *Varied Types*. This was originally published in 1902 and underwent several editions.

83. Chesterton, *A Handful of Authors*. This is a posthumous collection of essays edited by Chesterton's assistant Dorothy Collins and published in 1953.

84. Chesterton, *A Handful of Authors*, 149.

85. See the "Conclusion" to Pater's most famous work *The Renaissance*, which I discuss below.

86. Collins, *A Handful of Authors*, 150. Note my discussion of the toy theater in the conclusion to this book. It is a significant and recurring theme in Chesterton's work.

constricted expansiveness, a point of eternity, a micro-cosmos, in which the viewer may engage in serious, childlike play.

So Chesterton had thought much about Ruskin, but he was also very familiar with the writings and views of Walter Pater and Oscar Wilde, frequently critiquing them in his books and essays. In addition, several of Chesterton's friends, including writers such as Max Beerbohm,[87] were the personal friends or disciples of Pater and Wilde, which perhaps led to Chesterton's tone of familiarity. In a 1909 *Daily News* article later collected in *A Handful of Authors*, Chesterton gives a sustained analysis, which is both critical and sympathetic, of Oscar Wilde. He writes,

> But while he had a strain of humbug in him . . . he had, in his own strange way, a much deeper and more spiritual nature than they. Queerly enough, it was the very multitude of his falsities that prevented him from being entirely false. Like a many-coloured humming top, he was at once a bewilderment and a balance. He was so fond of being many-sided that among his sides he even admitted the right side. He loved so much to multiply his souls that he had among them one soul at least that was saved. He desired all beautiful things—even God.[88]

Like his estimation of Ruskin, Chesterton also has issues with many of Wilde's ideas. Yet he also gives him a most sympathetic reading. Full essays, book chapters, and other smaller references dealing with Pater and Wilde abound in Chesterton's many works.[89] Moreover, Chesterton

87. Beerbohm (1872–1956) was a gifted caricaturist, a critic, and a short-story author who was involved with the English avant-garde circles during the *fin de siècle*; see Drabble, *Oxford Companion to English Literature*, 80.

88. Collins, *A Handful of Authors*, 146.

89. *Heretics*, Chesterton's popular 1905 collection of essays, contains an entire chapter, "Omar and the Sacred Vine," which discusses the general philosophical outlook of both Pater and Wilde. Chesterton's criticisms here are insightful and witty as always: "Many of the most brilliant intellects of our time have urged us to the same self-conscious snatching at a rare delight. Walter Pater said that we were all under sentence of death, and the only course was to enjoy exquisite moments simply for those moments' sake. The same lesson was taught by the very powerful and very desolate philosophy of Oscar Wilde. It is the *carpe diem* religion; but the *carpe diem* religion is not the religion of happy people, but of very unhappy people. Great joy does not gather the rosebuds while it may; its eyes are fixed on the immortal rose which Dante saw." Later he writes, "[Happy] moments are filled with eternity; these moments are joyful because they do not seem momentary. Once look at them as moments after Pater's manner, and they become as cold as Pater and his style. Man cannot love mortal things. He can only love immortal things for an instant." See Chesterton, *Heretics*, 102, 108–9.

frequently deals with other writers he deems to be part of this "art for art's sake" sensibility, such as the American painter James McNeill Whistler.[90] These are far too numerous to completely list here, but just as I mentioned earlier in regard to Chesterton's interaction with Ruskin, all of these references show that Chesterton was a continual reader and critic of Pater and Wilde as well. Given Chesterton's immense popularity, prolific output, and contemporary influence, it is indeed significant that a great deal of Chesterton's early writings, both articles and books, are directly concerned with matters of art, British painters, aesthetic ideas, and the continuing influence of these three Victorian critics.

The Scope of This Book

In what follows I divide this work into three chapters on the three substantial *fin-de-siècle* aesthetic approaches to religion. In my close readings I will show how these Victorian minds sought, in the latter half of the century, to recover some sense of religious meaning by means of aesthetic experience. I argue that the attempted recoveries by Ruskin and Pater—which I summarize as *theoria* and *aesthesis*—are two possible positions that attempt to find some relationship between beauty and God.

In the first chapter I outline Ruskin's aesthetic philosophy as it is creatively and beautifully put forward in his *Modern Painters I* and II. I will demonstrate how it was a two-fold attempt to root beauty in the action of God and then to demonstrate something about God through beauty. This experience of God through beauty is possible because of loving aesthetic perception, which Ruskin calls "the theoretic faculty," or more simply, "theoria." It is then the role of artists, according to Ruskin's system, to communicate to others those messages of God that are scattered throughout nature. Perceptive critics such as Ruskin have the role to step in as mediators and interpreters of these artistic representations of God's speech. Ruskin's first two volumes of *Modern Painters* were enormously successful and popular, and together they constitute Ruskin's approach to

---

90. *Heretics* also contains a very critical chapter on the art of American painter James McNeill Whistler (1834–1903), titled "On the Wit of Whistler." See Chesterton, *Heretics*, 234–46. John Ruskin furiously critiqued Whistler at several points of his career as well, famously being involved in a libel case against the American artist. In their mutual attack on Whistler's entire philosophy of art, Chesterton and Ruskin are yet again quite similar. See the fascinating account in Merrill, *A Pot of Paint, Aesthetics on Trial in Whistler v. Ruskin*. Also see Drabble, "Whistler," in *The Oxford Companion to English Literature*, 1061.

theological aesthetics and natural theology. However, I will also point out that Ruskin lacked a robust doctrine of flesh and incarnation in his system, and this will lead to some of the aesthetes' and Chesterton's critiques.

In the second chapter I will lead the reader through important critical works by Walter Pater and Oscar Wilde, showing that their aesthetic ideas owe much to Ruskin, despite their radical departure from his Evangelicalism and his effort of rooting beauty in God. These aesthetes move toward an "art for art's sake" aesthetic alone. Yet, like Ruskin, even the "antinomians" Pater and Wilde display an obsession with Christian history, spirituality, and Scripture, trying to reach some sort of religion of beauty without the dogmatic and metaphysical baggage of "Christendom." In their "art for art's sake" aesthetic, they do recover a sense of the fleshly, incarnated beauty of things, but they lack any metaphysical foundation that might allow them to give an adequate account of what exactly makes flesh (or humanity) beautiful.

In the third chapter I argue that G. K. Chesterton, as he follows on the heels of these Victorian aesthetic and religious discussions, begins to make a name for himself just as these three are passing away.[91] Chesterton pulls together the approaches of Ruskin and the aesthetes, recognizing the presence of God in the natural world as well as the singular beauty of the human person. Where Chesterton goes beyond these three critical predecessors is in his disposition toward symbolism and the symbolist movement. I do not want to overstate my case: Chesterton was a popular journalist and was not a professional philosopher or academic. He dropped out of art school and never exhibited his own artworks in galleries, mostly reserving his caricatures and sketches for puppet shows for children, as well as to provide illustrations for several books written by friends, specifically Bentley and Belloc.[92] Yet in his work there is a bold and creative theological aesthetic that radically reevaluates Victorian aesthetics and presents the centrality of the *imago Dei*—the image of God—in the center of the human person who is a symbol of the Divine Artist: God.

91. Pater died in 1894; Ruskin and Wilde in 1900. Chesterton published his first essay in 1895 and a number of essays by 1900. See chapter 3 below.

92. Edmund Clerihew Bentley (1875–1956), who went to grammar school with Chesterton, was a journalist for the *Daily News* and *Daily Telegraph*. He's mainly remembered today for the humorous type of poem called a "clerihew." Hillaire Belloc (1870–1953) was a prolific author of poetry, novels, travelogues, and historical works. A close friend of Chesterton, they collaborated on various books and journals. See Drabble, *The Oxford Companion to English Literature*, 89, 84.

1

Theoria

John Ruskin's System

IN HIS *MODERN PAINTERS, Volume I, Containing Parts I and II: Of General Principles and of Truth* (1843),[1] Ruskin devotes hundreds of pages to his minute observations of natural phenomena. The patient, tireless observation combined with his soaring prose marks this young art critic's first published book as a masterpiece of style. For Ruskin, the loving inspection of every aspect of creation—each leaf and cloud, branch and stone—is the beginning of knowledge and the key to unlocking both the value and meaning of all art. It is no wonder that, with as wide a readership as it had, including the significant writers Charlotte Brontë and George Eliot, *Modern Painters* would make an enormous impact in Victorian Britain. It was just the first of many works that influenced landscape art, art criticism, the revival of the Gothic, and the eventual manifestation of the art nouveau movement.[2] On Ruskin (who wrote under the *nom de plume*, "a Graduate of Oxford" in *Modern Painters* volume I), Brontë says, "He writes like a consecrated Priest of the Abstract and Ideal," and Eliot writes, "I venerate him as one of the great teachers of the day" (MP

1. I use the standard "Library Edition" of Ruskin's works. *Modern Painters I* is found in volume 3: Cook and Wedderburn, *The Works of John Ruskin*, vol. 3. In order to avoid confusion, and because I give a close reading of this book throughout the chapter, I hereafter parenthetically cite this third volume of the Library Edition, containing all of *Modern Painters Volume I*, as (MP I, page #).

2. Herbert, *The Art Criticism of John Ruskin*, xxx.

I, xxxix). This "Priest" and "great teacher" who wrote with such brilliant insight and beautiful style was not yet twenty-five years old, and yet he left an indelible mark on British aesthetics, culture, and the imagination.

What was it exactly about *Modern Painters*, with the "Oxford Graduate's" precise notes on everything from clouds to grass blades that exerted such influence on the writers, poets, and artists of Britain in the mid-nineteenth century? What was this particular art critic's creed that was so captivating, especially to an Oxford graduate named Walter Pater and a young university student named Oscar Wilde?

Ruskin's theory of art, which he later calls "theoria" in volume II of *Modern Painters*, is an overtly Christian aesthetic, steeped in what is traditionally called "natural theology," yet answering different questions than such a theological discipline.[3] For Ruskin's purpose is neither to prove the existence of God as such nor to provide a theodicy, that is, a defense of God's goodness in the face of contradictory evidence; his purpose is, rather, to demonstrate that beauty is a channel for the goodness and love of what can only be a Creator God. Through aesthetic experiences, truths of God's attributes reach the heart of the beholder. Then, in a move that might surprise contemporary readers, Ruskin argues that

---

3. Yet, since Ruskin's death in 1901, very few theologians or religious studies scholars have taken his Christian-colored aesthetics very seriously. Some notable exceptions include the fine 2017 study by Aidan Nichols, *All Great Art Is Praise: Art and Religion in John Ruskin*. There are also substantial reflections on Ruskin in George Pattison's excellent book *Art, Modernity, and Faith*, and a fascinating comparison of Darwin, Ruskin, and Scruton in Anthony O'Hear's *Transcendence, Creation, and Incarnation*. L. Clifton Edwards gives an admirable interpretation of Ruskin's "creational theology of natural beauty," in *Creation's Beauty as Revelation* from 2014. There is a more recent book of essays edited by Sheona Beaumont and Madeleine Emerald Thiele titled *John Ruskin, the Pre-Raphaelites, and Religious Imagination* released in Spring 2023—too late for me to utilize for this book. Other religious studies scholars such as David M. Craig in his book *John Ruskin and the Ethics of Consumption* have carried out valuable research into Ruskin's political economy, discovering within the art critic's voluminous writings many valuable political-ethical insights the current world would be wise to take into consideration. However, for the most part, a vast majority of the research into Ruskin's poetry, life, art, and political and aesthetic philosophy has been carried out by literary critics and historians. Yet at the popular level, even during Ruskin's lifetime, there were substantial conversations about Ruskin's religious beliefs. For example, there is a book of Bible quotations from Ruskin's voluminous works arranged by Mary and Ellen Gibbs. It underwent several editions; see Ruskin, *The Bible References in the Works of John Ruskin*. Ruskin's works have always been mined for their many soaring passages on ethics and religion, especially in new publications of compilations and anthologies.

the single greatest beholder who has received this message of God and passed it along is the landscape artist J. M. W. Turner.[4]

*Modern Painters I*s thus a kind of complex, multi-volume apology for the art of Turner, and yet, in his defense, Ruskin establishes an important aesthetic in Britain at this time which would inspire the other aesthetic movements during the century, such as "art for art's sake" and, ultimately, symbolism.[5]

Rather than summarize the entire first volume with many different arguments, I will instead focus my analysis upon three recurring theological-aesthetic loci. Ruskin was neither a philosopher nor a theologian, and yet his early and significant body of work is continuously engaged with Christian ideas. Keeping in mind the religious and aesthetic fabric of this century, I will be interpreting Ruskin as, at his core, concerned primarily with finding a place for his religion in the beauty of the natural world. His entire enterprise rests on the idea that earthly, material beauty corresponds to and communicates nonmaterial, spiritual truth. His project is, at its core, a theological one.

Beauty & Morality in *Modern Painters I*

Morality is central to Ruskin's theory of beauty, and in *Modern Painters*, both the perception and production of beauty stem from the moral center that God has given human beings. Even though one scholar, George Landow, has referred to his "theocentric system of ethics" in the book as "idiosyncratic, eclectic, and often puzzling,"[6] it is undeniable that God-centered moral perception forms a foundation for Ruskin's entire project. Despite his veiled critique, this same scholar has also helpfully traced Ruskin's understanding of morality back to Adam Smith, Edmund Burke, and the other moral philosophers, demonstrating that Ruskin understood "moral" to mean "ethical," and to include "all mental processes" of human

---

4. J. M. W. Turner (1775–1851) was a British landscape artist who traveled extensively throughout England, France, Italy, and Switzerland. Many of his works depict the action of nature: storms, snows, fires, etc. Ruskin wrote *Modern Painters* volume I to defend his work against his many detractors. See Drabble, *The Oxford Companion to English Literature*, 1006–7.

5. See Warner and Hough, *Strangeness and Beauty*, 1:13.

6. Landow, *The Aesthetic and Critical Theories of John Ruskin*, 110. Note that Landow is not a theologian but a literary scholar, primarily of the Victorian Age.

beings.[7] Whether or not Ruskin's system of ethics is "often puzzling," one thing is certain; in the aesthetics of beauty, morality is an ever-present force; it allows for the true interpretation of the messages of God written across the natural world.

Ruskin believes that both good creation and true perception come from a human's moral center. To create beauty or to appreciate it, one must be morally pure. The intellect is not sufficient to grasp beauty, for a "material object which can give us pleasure in the simple contemplation of its outward qualities without any direct and definite exertion of the intellect, I call in some way, or in some degree, beautiful" (MP I, 109). The beautiful affects a person's heart, feelings, and spirit—not simply her or his mental activities. To be truly changed by this beauty then, one must have moral good taste: "Perfect taste is the faculty of receiving the greatest possible pleasure from those material sources which are attractive to our moral nature in its purity and perfection" (MP I, 110).

This moral good taste allows for the reception of the messages of God through beauty in the natural world. Perception without moral nature—that is, without gratitude, love, and appreciation—becomes an empty looking. In a particularly rich passage in which he discusses moral sensibility, Ruskin writes, "I believe this kind of sensibility may be entirely resolved into the acuteness of bodily sense of which I have been speaking, associated with love, love I mean in its infinite and holy functions, as it embraces divine and human and brutal intelligences, and hallows the physical perception of external objects by association, gratitude, veneration, and other pure feelings of our moral nature" (MP I, 143). He goes on to say that "a man of deadened moral sensation is always dull in his perception of truth" (MP I, 143). Ruskin means that morality allows an apprehension of truth, and that apprehension strengthens the beholder's moral fiber.

It is this hallowed perception, stemming from a moral center, that makes a great artist. Education and reputation have nothing to do with it. To copy style rather than nature is to become a "parrot painter" (MP I,156). For it is only the moral center that prepares an artist to approach her or his task with the proper love and veneration. One finds the means to create beauty by it: "The teaching of nature is as varied and infinite as it is constant; and the duty of the painter is to watch for every one of her lessons, and to give (for human life will admit of nothing more) those in

7. Landow, *The Aesthetic and Critical Theories of John Ruskin*, 157.

which she has manifested each of her principles in the most peculiar and striking way" (MP I, 156). Then Ruskin declares, "All really great pictures, therefore, exhibit the general habits of nature, manifested in some peculiar, rare, and beautiful way" (MP I, 157). The general habits of nature are not random characteristics due to chaos or chance; they are, rather, the carefully ordered phenomena that illustrate the goodness and will of God, always for the benefit of each perceiving creature. This means that nature which is from God is ever truthful. It is the artist's duty to pass along this truth, which, ultimately, is a message from a Divine Benefactor.

Beauty & Truth in *Modern Painters I*

To demonstrate the seriousness with which Ruskin treats natural phenomena, I will now focus upon two chapters which are illustrative of the whole work. Ruskin devotes two entire chapters, which make up more than sixty pages (in the Library Edition), as well as many other paragraphs scattered throughout the work, simply to the "truth of clouds." These chapters are situated in the middle of Ruskin's organizational pattern of volume I; in turn he treats skies, clouds, earth, central mountains, inferior mountains, foreground rocks, water, and vegetation, demonstrating to the reader how the old landscape artists—those masters of the Dutch and Flemish schools as well as more recent English artists—have consistently failed to interpret God's gift of nature with any fidelity. In this failure to accurately paint natural scenes on the canvas, Ruskin shows such artists' popularity in the Royal Academy is entirely unwarranted.

Regrettably, there is another artist who has been accused of telling fanciful lies despite his great fidelity to the truths of nature: Turner. Ruskin changes the aesthetic conversation to one thing about Turner: his *truthfulness*. If he can prove that Turner is telling the truth in his paintings while the various popular artists in England are telling lies, then he can prove that this painter is the greatest of all. After some lengthy introductory chapters dealing with first principles and Joshua Reynolds's lectures on art, Ruskin writes,

> I shall endeavor, therefore, in the present portion of the work, to enter with care and impartiality into the investigation of the claims of the schools in ancient and modern landscape to faithfulness in representing nature. I shall pay no regard whatsoever to what may be thought beautiful, or sublime, or imaginative. I shall look only for truth: bare, clear, down-right statement of

> facts; showing in each particular, as far as I am able, what the truth of nature is, and then seeking for the plain expression of it, and for that alone. And I shall thus endeavor, totally regardless of fervour of imagination or brilliancy of effect, or any other of their more captivating qualities, to examine and to judge the works of the great living painter, who is, I believe, imagined by the majority of the public, to paint more falsehood and less fact than any other known master. We shall see with what reason.[8]

Ruskin is not concerned with originality or greatness of style in painting. The reputation of such masters as Joshua Reynolds[9] and Poussin[10] does not silence his harsh critique of their imaginative errors in painting. Ruskin is interested in one thing: *truth*. Natural truth—that is, fidelity to nature—is also, for Ruskin, *theological* truth. The messages from God in nature are not to be destroyed or modified, but rather, lovingly and accurately re-presented. This is Ruskin's guiding, foundational principle, and his entire aesthetic is built upon the uncovering of this truth through the arts. His task to find truth and Turner's task to paint truth is, naturally, a moral endeavor.

For Turner as for Ruskin, landscape art must be "a witness to the omnipotence of God" (MP I, 22). In this stout first volume Ruskin is establishing a God-centered aesthetic, where nature and art continually do the work of theology, pointing to the role and attributes of a Heavenly Father. That is, both the beauty of the natural world and that beauty translated onto an artist's canvas can inspire or convict mankind and then teach various things about God. In his great wisdom God even intends for the arts to effect his purposes. Returning to one of Ruskin's many themes, clouds, it will now be helpful to track his arguments in support of faithful cloud-observation, appreciation, and then rendering.

The reader of the two cloud chapters in *Modern Painters* will learn much about the technical aspects of cloud-painting and on the many failures of the English, Dutch, and Flemish landscape artists of the past

8. MP I, 138–39.

9. Reynolds (1723–92), author of *Fifteen Discourses to the Royal Academy* which were published talks of his from the 1760s through the 1780s, taught that "Artists should follow the rules derived from studying the great masters of the past, especially those who worked in the classical tradition; art should generalize to create the universal rather than the particular," etc. See Stokstad and Cateforis, *Art History*, 920.

10. Nicolas Poussin (1594–1665) was influential in his ordering of landscape elements, painting not what was visible or realistic but what was the ordered, classical ideal. See Stokstad and Cateforis, *Art History*, 745.

two centuries. Ruskin devotes dozens of pages to both the glories of the clouds and the inglorious way most artists who were considered great in their day utterly failed to capture their glorious beauty. Of course, their beauty reveals the infinity and majesty of God, who dwells in the heavens.

Therefore, painting anything from nature is certainly no small undertaking. Ruskin wastes no time in setting out his thesis of these chapters: "There is but one master whose works we can think of while we read this, one alone has taken notice of the neglected upper sky; it is his peculiar and favorite field; he has watched its every modification, and given its every phase and feature; at all hours, in all seasons, he has followed its passions and its changes, and has brought down and laid open to the world another apocalypse of Heaven" (MP I, 363). Clouds, in their ever-evolving, complex and multifaceted beauty, have been traced by God in the sky for humanity's moral and spiritual benefit; they are not trifling amusements for artists to fancifully manipulate. Ruskin actually refers to clouds themselves as the "apocalypse of heaven" (MP I, 363) and he writes about the many "truths connected with them" (MP I, 369). These truths are sublime ones that direct humanity's praise to a loving Creator God.

It follows that any artistic representation of clouds should seek to present such lessons with fidelity, lest the original truth from God should become lost in an inaccurate, subjective interpretation, or worse, a downright lie. Ruskin has no patience for those artists who depart from nature; any falsehood in art is wrong because "falsehood is in itself revolting and degrading . . . and because nature is so immeasurably superior to all that the human mind can conceive, that every departure from her is a fall beneath her . . ." (MP I, 137). And so it is that bad art, like bad architecture, is more than just an annoyance or eyesore. Bad art is an affront to the moral sense for it violates the very truth that God is displaying via his natural world. A painter must approach the task of painting as a teacher of the church approaches the task of commenting upon the sacred Word (MP I, 157). If this other sacred Word, this nature-scripture, is misrepresented or portrayed in an untruthful way, then the artist is not just a bad and therefore untalented artist, but a bad person in a moral and religious way. God has created all things, and in the language of Genesis 1 and *Modern Painters*, God has seen his creation to be good. It is so good that the artists who would wish to ignore it to follow their personal fancies no longer proclaim fully the goodness of the Creator God. They and their productions are immoral. Ruskin will excuse honest mistakes, made in ignorance, but he will not tolerate dishonest mistakes, for in his aesthetics such mistakes are made in willful rebellion against God's "Book of Nature."[11]

In these cloud chapters Ruskin again misses no opportunity to catalogue the inaccurate follies he finds in the older landscape school, represented especially by the Baroque school and the painters Nicolas Poussin and Claude Lorrain,[12] and he thereby shows to the reader what are ultimately spiritual weaknesses and moral deceits. Artists who remain truthful with their clouds, who approach natural clouds with reverence and openness, wishing to learn about God, will be powerful communicators of his providence, power, and love. This is why Ruskin is able to complete his chapter on clouds in a great praise of the one truthful, faithful, earthly artist he has come to defend: J. M. W. Turner.

> The conclusion, then, to which we are led by our present examination of the truth of clouds is, that the old masters attempted the representation of only one among the thousands of their systems of scenery, and were altogether false in the little they attempted; while we can find records in modern art of every form or phenomenon of the heavens from the highest film that glorifies the aether to the wildest vapour that darkens the dust, and in all these records, we find the most clear language and close thought, firm words and true message, unstinted fulness and unfailing faith.[13]

Far from lessening the worth of Turner's art by endlessly connecting it to God and the study of theology, Ruskin affords it a place higher than any other critic before or since has dared to give it. When art does become, as with Ruskin, a means of communicating the divine Truth to others, it becomes a moral, sacred task. This turns the painter into a prophet, the critic into the artist's scribe. It is Ruskin's task as such a scribe to defend and propagate the message of God's revelation that has been given to Turner. Ruskin does his work through a medium faithful to the beauty of the original revelation and the faithful copy of the revelation: his carefully

11. Scholarly opinion is a bit divided on the origin of this striking phrase, but it seems as if St. Augustine was the first to compare God's Word in the Bible with God's Word in creation, thus, there are "two books" of the one Divine Author. See Juurikkala, "The Two Books of God," 1.

12. Claude Lorrain (1600–1682) was, along with Nicolas Poussin, a significant influence on painters of the following two centuries for his ideal, classical landscapes. See Stokstad and Cateforis, *Art History*, 745.

13. MP I, 415.

worded, detailed, and elevated prose. In what Ruskin later described as "perhaps the best and truest piece of work done in the first volume" (MP I, 419, footnote), he concludes his chapter on clouds with words about the colorful skies above a mountainous landscape. This eloquent passage in the present volume follows a thorough deconstruction of Claude's method of painting clouds. The crescendo is this:

> And then wait yet for one hour, until the east again becomes purple . . . : watch the white glaciers blaze in their winding paths about the mountains, like mighty serpents with scales of fire: watch the columnar peaks of solitary snow, kindling downwards, chasm by chasms, each in itself a new morning; their long avalanches cast down in keen streams brighter than the lightning, sending each his tribute of driven snow, like altar-smoke, up to the heaven, . . . and then, when you can look no more for gladness, and when you are bowed down with fear and love of the Maker and Doer of this, tell me who has best delivered this His message unto men![14]

Ruskin is capable of such lofty praise of Turner because, in Ruskin's estimation, if art is to be religious, it need not specifically involve biblical characters or stories, Christian saints or legends. In fact, religious art for Ruskin (and for Turner) is something much more elementary, or, one might say, elemental. Turner is "the only perfect landscape painter whom the world has ever seen" (MP I, 616) because he is the celebrant of the very elements of creation: the mountains and clouds, trees and skies that make up the holy clouds, skies, and hills that, for Ruskin, function explicitly like Scripture verses. Turner is therefore a religious artist in the truest sense, for he has seen the truth of the Lord and has re-presented it to others.

Beauty & God in *Modern Painters I*

As a mid-century Evangelical Christian, Ruskin's knowledge of the Old and New Testaments was exceptional. His writing is peppered with references to biblical types.[15] The Ruskin scholar George Landow, in his work *Victorian Types, Victorian Shadows*, points out that, essentially, Ruskin's

14. MP I, 418–19.

15. See Ruskin, *The Bible References in the Works of John Ruskin*. This book is arranged alphabetically by key word to allow the reader to quickly find what Ruskin had to say about various scriptural personages, events, and themes.

entire endeavor in *Modern Painters* is to show that nature contains *types* of the attributes of God; or, in other words, that "all phenomena which we find beautiful, such as proportioned curves, symmetry, and pure colors, act as a type of divinity."[16] In his work specifically on Ruskin's aesthetics, Landow makes an important distinction between "type" and "allegory," and shows that Ruskin had a typological understanding of creation rather than an allegorical one. Typology respects the historical timeframe whereas allegories lift things out of time; "In other words, whereas a type focuses attention on both its historical existence and its meaning, an allegory places most importance on its significance."[17] In the post-Romantic era, Ruskin finds a foundation for his faith in these natural types. Apart from the any liturgical, sacramental tradition, even apart from Jesus Christ, Ruskin sees God the Father's mark in the earthly types found in nature.

In this first volume of *Modern Painters* Ruskin is most concerned with connecting beauty, painting, creativity, imagination—in short, every aspect of aesthetics considered from above and below—as integral to humans' relationship with God. This relation is necessarily moral; it is in the right response to the appearance of God's attributes through nature that human beings can be truthful artists and beholders, filled with love and gratitude. Yet the previous sections have also hinted at something else regarding Ruskin's view of God; it is focused squarely upon a certain idea of God.

Ruskin's concept of *theoria* is strictly concerned with God as Father and Creator. Ruskin is most interested in humanity's natural ability to discover God as a loving and powerful Deity whose attributes can be glimpsed through proper attention to his many earthly types. This human ability allows human beings to perceive, appreciate, and love God. The natural power to see the Creator in what he has created is the key to all things for Ruskin, and since God tells no lies, then neither does his chosen means of communication: nature. Ruskin readily describes "that faultless, ceaseless, inconceivable, inexhaustible loveliness, which God has stamped upon all things"; we then must be "ready to receive them as He gives them" (MP I, 48). These nature-scriptures, like the Holy Scriptures, express God's thoughts and desires for humankind.

16. Landow, *Victorian Types, Victorian Shadows*, 216.

17. Landow, *The Aesthetic and Critical Theories of John Ruskin*, 350.

To recapitulate, these are Ruskin's theological-aesthetic conclusions of his first, impressive volume; firstly, whereas priests, monks, or scholars are specially attuned to receive God's message from his written Scripture, artists are specially attuned to receive the word of God "from clouds, and leaves, and waves"; then just as religious people must practice what they read if they are to be truthful interpreters of the Bible, so must artists strive to keep natural truth unblemished if they wish to be good artists (MP I, 45). Secondly, this natural word does not replace the written word, but works alongside it as another aid: "We should use pictures not as authorities, but as comments on nature, just as we use divines not as authorities, but as comments on the Bible" (MP I, 45, footnote). Thirdly, because of his fidelity to nature as God has actually created it, J. M. W. Turner is the painter *par excellence* and in his deeply truthful paintings he has become a prophet, a chosen proclaimer of God's Word, which is now expansively presented to the viewing public.

In the next section I will track these same theological-aesthetic loci in Ruskin's second volume of *Modern Painters*. Despite the fact that Ruskin veers off the path of his original plan for the work, he is still seeking the same basic answer to his deeply theological question: how is our art related to the art—that is, the creation—of God? As I will demonstrate, Ruskin is able to once again discover a Providential Father figure in heaven, yet cannot find a place in his aesthetic for earthy, fleshly humanity. Similar to his first volume, the God Ruskin presents in his second volume typically appears somewhat impersonal and abstract, and there is very little place for the incarnation of God and its consequences for human creativity.

Modern Painters II

Modern Painters, Volume II is, in several respects, a surprisingly different sort of work than the first volume.[18] One might expect to find in this book further reflections on natural phenomena: rocks, hills, rivers, trees, and other things, with a slightly older and more famous graduate of Oxford continuing to argue for Turner's place as head of the landscape artists of the day. Instead, there is a significant change of direction, with Ruskin taking a different approach to Turner and the other modern landscape

18. Cook and Wedderburn, *The Works of John Ruskin*, vol. 4. Hereafter I will parenthetically cite this work, which contains all of *Modern Painters II*, as (MP II, page #) in my text.

painters than he did previously. Indeed, volume II is really an extended, theoretical treatise on beauty, imagination, and truth, examined through Ruskin's brilliant interpretations of Italian medieval and Renaissance artists. The young critic still practices those outstanding observational powers of his, but he turns them upon the classic (though at the time, mostly overlooked) early Florentine and Venetian masters whose paintings he discovered on moldering monastery walls and inside forgotten chapels. Two events made Ruskin change his original plan for the volume: first, his reading A. F. Rio's book on Christian art, *De La Poesie Chretienne dans son principe, dans sa matiere et dans ses formes* (1836), and second, his impactful trip to Venice, Pisa, and Florence, where he experienced those powerful works of the fourteenth- and fifteenth-century Italians (MP II, xxiii). His editors write, "His interest in this book, quickened by his studies in the Louvre, determined him to revisit Italy and study the early Christian painters before proceeding any further with his essay. The tour of 1845 was the decisive factor in making the second volume what it is, and was also the turning point in Ruskin's career" (MP II, xxiii–xxiv).

Ruskin was changed by the art he gazed upon during this Italian tour. The beauty and power of these early Renaissance works moved Ruskin to further develop his concept of beauty. In his new, more overtly philosophical endeavor to explain aesthetic experience, Ruskin develops one of his most important concepts: that of the *theoretic faculty*.[19] The theoretic faculty, or simply *theoria*, is that contemplative ability, coming from the heart, that is concerned with approaching and understanding beauty in its moral depth and complexity (MP II, 35ff). Theoria is therefore deeply penetrative and faithful perception. If "aesthesis" is the sensory experience of a thing's outward surface with an appreciation of its physical qualities, then theoria is the experience of a thing's outward beauty and inward truth in the fullness of its relations. It takes a pure heart to receive beauty and the message of God in beauty (MP II, 35). Indeed, along with the careful and studious act of looking, a kind of reverence is required from the observer. Then what precisely is beauty in Ruskin's system? As we have also seen in his first volume, Ruskin will reiterate here that beauty is that which stirs the heart and awakens the spirit; it is that divine loveliness that reveals the very attributes of God (MP II, 144).

19. Taken from the Greek verb θεωρέω. Ruskin defines this as "I discern, I see mentally." It is an interpretive, contemplative action and not merely an outward, visual, aesthetic experience. See MP II, 42.

Beauty & Morality in *Modern Painters II*

Morality is linked to beauty in at least three major ways. The first is that in the theoretic faculty's perception of beauty, one must have the "moral retina" along with the "intellectual lens" to perceive rightly (MP II, 35). The second link is to the imagination itself; no artist can produce true art unless he or she cultivates the right moral feelings. These two insights were once again made by Ruskin when he was before the frescoes of the Campo Santo in Pisa and the works found in the great Florentine churches. The early Renaissance artists who executed these works were morally excellent not simply because they painted religious subject matter, but rather because they approached all subject matter in this moral way; they were filled with reverence for the beautiful things of God, and so they were able to produce beautiful things in return (MP II, 30). The third link of morality to beauty is of a structural, compositional nature; Ruskin writes, "The beauty of the animal form is in exact proportion to the amount of moral or intellectual virtue expressed in it" (MP II, 160).

Integral to this moral view of beauty is the concept of theoria, where aesthetic perception is intertwined with the powers of the human heart. Looking at the second chapter, "Of the Theoretic Faculty," we see that §8 is aptly summarized as *"Ideas of Beauty, how essentially moral."* Ruskin argues here that his ideas of beauty are "the subject of moral, and not of intellectual, nor altogether of sensual perception" (MP II, 48). The sensual pleasure of beauty must always come first, as is proven by experience. "[I]t is necessary to the existence of an idea of beauty, that the sensual pleasure which may be its basis should be accompanied first with joy, then with love of the object, then with the perception of kindness in a superior intelligence, finally, with thankfulness and veneration towards that intelligence itself . . ." (MP II, 48). The pleasure is accompanied with joy and love, and then after a perception of God, one responds to beauty with the biblical responses of thankfulness and praise.[20] This right kind of aesthetic (theoretic) perception is further tied to *purity of taste.* By this Ruskin does not mean bourgeois, cultural sophistication, and he certainly is not suggesting that there is only one type of style in art that is acceptable. Rather, he means that beauty is so universally experienced by those of pure heart and conscience that that constitutes pure taste. Pure taste is taste that is unspotted by sin, baseness, or pride:

20. For example, Psalm 100.

> But if we can perceive beauty in everything of God's doing, we may argue that we have reached the true perception of its universal laws. Hence, false taste may be known by its fastidiousness, by its demands of pomp, splendour, and unusual combination, by its enjoyment only of particular styles and modes of things, and by its pride also. . . . But true taste is forever growing, learning, reading, worshipping, laying its hand upon its mouth because it is astonished, lamenting over itself, and testing itself by the way that it fits things.[21]

This is an important point, for in this sense is art related to morality: not that art teaches humanity to become moral, but that art can only be produced in the first place by moral humanity, so that along with taste then comes certain effects—negative or positive—which reveal the nature of that moral or immoral taste of both artist and beholder. Both pure taste and false taste are therefore proven by their respective fruits.[22] This is the second way that morality is linked with aesthetics: the moral or immoral nature of artists. Beautiful art is produced by women and men who have a strong moral basis and are not led astray by lies or pomp: "No supreme power of art can be attained by impious men" (MP II, 211). Even though evil artists are capable of painting very beautiful works and sculpting very moving statues, they are to be compared to the spirit of prophecy given to Balaam or Saul despite their sins (MP II, 214). Ruskin writes, "It seems to me that much of what is great, and to all men beneficial, has been wrought by those who neither intended nor knew the good they did, and that many mighty harmonies have been discoursed by instruments that had been dumb or discordant, but that God knew their stops"[23] (MP II, 213–14).

Beauty & Truth in *Modern Painters II*

Ruskin makes an important distinction between beauty and truth in this second volume, a distinction that clarifies much of his earlier volume's remarks on nature being both beautiful and true at the same time. In chapter IV, "Of False Opinions Held Concerning Beauty," Ruskin argues

21. MP II, 60.

22. See Matthew 7:17, 18: "So, every healthy tree bears good fruit, but the diseased tree bears bad fruit. A healthy tree cannot bear bad fruit, nor can a diseased tree bear good fruit."

23. Ruskin refers here to the stops of an organ.

against these three "erring" opinions: "the first, that the Beautiful is the True; the second, that the Beautiful is the Useful; the third, that it is dependent on Custom; and the fourth; that it is dependent on the Association with Ideas" (MP II, 66). I am mainly concerned with the first erring opinion discussed in this section. Ruskin argues that mingling the true with the beautiful is like mingling propositions with matter; it is a categorical mistake. Truth is different from beauty, but what is beautiful is almost always true as well, because ugliness often accompanies what is lying and false. Regarding the believers of this mistaken opinion Ruskin writes, "But giving the best and most rational interpretation we can, and supposing the holders of this strange position to mean only that things are beautiful which appear what they indeed are, and ugly which appear what they are not, we find them instantly contradicted by each and every conclusion of experience" (MP II, 66). He uses the example that a cloud can look less like a cloud and more like a castle, and in that resemblance to something else it is found to be beautiful. Ruskin is concerned with both beauty and truth in this volume, but he carefully notes here that they are not to be mingled. In arguing that the beautiful is not the true, Ruskin is saying that true representations of natural phenomena in art can nevertheless be dull, insipid, and evil, if there is no beauty, goodness, love, or repose. Truth qualifies beauty; beauty does not qualify (or determine) truth.

Yet, it might come with some surprise that Ruskin then has harsh words about the "horrid images of the Passion by which vulgar Romanism has always striven to excite the languid sympathies of its untaught flocks" (MP II, 201). Such "horrid pictures" do not uncover truth below the surface but, to Ruskin at least, manipulate the emotions of the Roman Catholic Church's "untaught flocks" by dwelling on the imperfect, the violent, and the sinful. In Ruskin's theoria, beauty must be untouched by any stain of sin or imperfection. In a sense, beauty is then a purified and idealistic thing.[24]

It is this emphasis on beauty that Pater and Wilde draw from in their early careers while modifying the overtly theological nature of Ruskinian beauty. Theoria is, by its very nature, more than just seeing for one's enjoyment; it is, rather, the combination of seeing with spiritual and moral sight, which accompanies physical sight. It is a penetrative, contemplative exercise that only human beings can practice as they are

24. This is an important theme that will be taken up in my final section on beauty and God in *Modern Painters II.*

the unique crown of God's creation and are especially equipped to sense God through the things he has made, and, after sensing, to pattern these sensations through their own artworks (MP II, 35). Artists use their imagination not to "exhibit things as they are not," but to faithfully represent in another medium those truths that have been received through the natural medium.

Beauty & God in Modern Painters II

Ruskin organizes the four ways that supernatural beings manifest themselves to human sense in time and history into the following categories:

1. External types, such as the flaming bush of the third chapter of Exodus

2. Symbolic forms, such as the Holy Spirit taking the form of a dove

3. Forms adopted but not necessarily seen, as the Risen Christ behind locked doors

4. Influence on human form, such as the shining face of Moses (MP II, 314–15).

Humanity experiences these manifestations through the Scriptures and also through artworks by faithful artists; these demonstrate the same kind of truth and beauty.

Ruskin's theory of typology is more explicit in this second volume than it is in the first. As we saw in the previous section on *Modern Painters I*, types are historical people, events, objects, and institutions that suggest or outline, in some sense, their corresponding antitypes. It is the antitype that fulfills the original, symbolic meaning of the type. It is in typology, in contradistinction to allegory, that the historical and physical reality of the type is crucial to its fulfillment in the present or future. Ruskin widens this definition of typology to include natural, mineralogical, and geological phenomena under the category of types; these natural things, too, have a history, a materiality, and they point to equally true facts about divine things; "[The] second means of obtaining supernatural character is that with which we are now concerned, namely, retaining the actual form in its full and material presence, and, without aid from any external interpretation whatsoever, to raise that form by mere inherent dignity to such pitch and power and impressiveness as cannot but assert and stamp it for superhuman" (MP II, 315–16).

Each element of the natural world, from the cleavage of a cliff to the vein structure of a leaf, is a natural wonder worthy of observation, study, and praise. In short, these natural things are also types, not gaining their meaning from some correspondence to Old Testament themes, but rather gaining their meaning from their symbolic and aesthetic purpose in God's creation. They stand alongside the institutions, persons, and events of the Scriptures as further modes of revelation available to the Creator. Yet Ruskin does not engage in flights of fancy when he relates the natural world and its wonders to lessons about God. For example, he does not hold that each type of stone or each variety of tree is a code or cypher that simply and directly indicates a different attribute of God. Rather, he teaches that the types found in nature make humanity open to theological truths: suggesting, guiding, directing, and teaching them. Thus in *Modern Painters II* we see a young John Ruskin still engaged in his natural theological program, without greatly changing the stance on typology and history that he establishes in the first volume.

Ruskin's intriguing observations in this volume, so devoted to the artists of sacred works he encountered in places such as the Campo Santo in Pisa and the San Marco monastery in Florence, are made in connection with the same concern for the truth of God that he made in the first volume. *Modern Painters II* is a thoroughly theological work because virtually every page is concerned with the discernment of God through the *theoretic* perception of beauty (MP II, 51). Ruskin writes, "But if we can perceive beauty in everything of God's doing, we may argue that we have reached the true perception of its universal laws" (MP II, 60). Ruskin then argues that these creations were most faithfully interpreted by the Italians of old who approached nature, history, and humanity with pious reverence and love.[25] These works must be seen again for they have lessons to teach: "[T]he neglect of art, as an interpreter of divine things, has been of evil consequence to the Christian world" (MP II, 211). Like in *Modern Painters I*, Ruskin's theological concern is with the Creator God, the Heavenly Father who dwells in the highest heavens yet provides paths to his children in the nature all around them so that they might come to know him. These natural paths could be anything found in nature, but absolutely every beautiful thing must, by its loveliness, reflect the traits of a beneficent Father.

25. Notice Ruskin's pivot from Turner; it is not as if Ruskin has forgotten Turner, but rather, since *Modern Painters I* he has come to discover the role of these early Renaissance Italians in the history of art, and thus, of humanity's relation to God's beauty.

But here, as in the previous volume, we again see that Ruskin is most concerned with the natural revelation of God the Father. In his project Ruskin simply is not concerned with Jesus—the fleshly embodiment of God, that is, God incarnated for humanity's sake. Ruskin's project takes place entirely in the territory of God's providence in creation and not his action of redemption. *Modern Painters* is a natural theological endeavor and Ruskin is explicit about this, but in it God ever seems a distant Father and Force rather than an intimate, incarnated person. In an illustrative passage Ruskin writes,

> But there is one thing that [distance] has, or suggests, which no other object of sight suggests in equal degree, and that is—Infinity. It is of all visible things the least material, the least finite, the most typical of the nature of God, the most suggestive of the glory of His dwelling-place. For the sky of night, though we may know it boundless, is dark; it is a studded vault, a roof that seems to shut us in and down; but the bright distance has no limit, we feel its infinity, as we rejoice in its purity of light.[26]

Distance, infinity, brightness—Ruskin gives us a glimpse at the glory of the God of the high heavens who alone is immortal and "dwells in unapproachable light."[27]

In a journal entry made in Italy (and included by the editors in *Modern Painters, Volume II*), Ruskin records his organizational pattern for all the religious art he had encountered in Italy. Broadly speaking, Ruskin finds there to be four classes of religious art, under which most if not all of the medieval-Renaissance painters find their place. The first class is that of "Pure Religious Art: The School of Love," and it includes those early Renaissance painters who were, in Ruskin's view, as saintly as they were artistic: Fra Angelico, Perugino, Duccio, Pinturicchio, and a few others (MP II, xxxiv–xxxv). The other three classes are "The School of the Great Men," "The School of Painting as Such," and "The School of Errors and Vices."[28] Ruskin shows that, though such artists painted nature in a

26. MP II, 81.

27. From 1 Timothy 6:16.

28. In class 2 Ruskin places Michelangelo, Giotto, Orcagna, Benozzo, and others who perceive nature with a religious feeling. In class 3 Ruskin places the great colorists who were not necessarily overtly religious—men such as Titian, Giorgione, and Bellini. Then in class 4 Ruskin considers Raphael (which he spells as "Rafaelle") in his later years to be particularly bad, morally and therefore artistically, along with Carracci and others. See Ruskin, *MP* II, xxxv–xxxvii.

technique that differs from Turner's, they nevertheless approached nature in the same way: with the utmost reverence and praise of the Creator. The early Renaissance works therefore are excellent examples of purity in art by which the divine traits of the Creator can be apprehended from the brushstrokes, colors, and overall treatment of subject. Though Ruskin, at this point of his life an Evangelical Christian, certainly confessed belief in Christ, the crucifixion, and all other major Christian doctrines, still, in the *Modern Painters* project, the place of Christ is lacking. The system of theoria does not actively need the very "image" of God who manifests God's glory in his body.[29] Rather, it is in natural phenomena that God reveals himself, specifically to the properly educated critic or artist who is able to notice him.

Even though Ruskin handles the early Renaissance masters in this second volume and leaves aside, for the moment, Turner and the other "modern painters," he by no means departs from his overriding concern throughout the work. The concern is the artists' fidelity to nature's truths and the beauties that display the attributes of the Creator. But Ruskin does wish to deal with the human form and the human flesh, especially if it is marred, bloodstained, or twisted. "Of Vital Beauty" and "Of the Superhuman Ideal" are the two most crucial chapters for understanding Ruskin's view of God and the human flesh.

"Of Vital Beauty" is concerned with further explanations of the concept, along with a glance at the list of works that particularly exhibit artistic powerlessness and impiety (MP II, 200). After citing works by Salvator Rosa and Orcagna, Ruskin references, almost in passing, that all "the horrible images of Passion, by which vulgar Romanism has always striven to excite the languid sympathies of its untaught flocks" are "most foul and detestable" (MP II, 200–201). Which "horrible images of [the] Passion" does Ruskin have in mind? Surely not such moving works as Fra Angelico's Crucifixion in San Marco or Cimabue's Cross in the Santa Croce? Ruskin explains his views further, "Of which foulness let us reason no farther, the very image and memory of them being pollution; only noticing this, that there has always been a morbid tendency in Romanism towards the contemplation of bodily pain, owing to the attribution of saving power to it . . ." (MP II, 202).

It is *any* painting of a bloody Jesus Christ that Ruskin has a difficult time accepting. Is this because of his Victorian sensibilities? Or

29. See Colossians 1:15 and 1 Timothy 3:16.

his Evangelical upbringing? Let us allow him to continue his attack on Passion images, "which, like every other moral error, has been of fatal effect in art, leaving not altogether without the stain and blame of it, even the highest of the Romanist painters; as Fra Angelico for instance, who, in his Passion subjects, always insists weakly on the bodily torture, and is unsparing of blood" (MP II, 202). Ruskin will not change his mind; any fresco with a hint of violence, death, or suffering is a polluting image because it sullies the pure perfection of God, as is glimpsed through the purity of nature. Ruskin continues his critique, this time considering Giotto: "[H]is treatment is usually grander, as in that Crucifixion over the door of the Convent of St. Mark's, where the blood is hardly actual, but issues from the feet in a conventional form, and becomes a crimson cord which is twined strangely beneath about a skull" (MP II, 202). If Ruskin prefers the blood of Christ to appear "hardly actual," what does he think of the real blood of Christ that dripped upon Calvary as the Gospels relate? Ruskin prefers a sanitized, idealized painting of Christ because a twisted and bloodied one does not fit within the confines of his system.

There are more examples that show Ruskin's view could not accommodate the human body in its brokenness and death. In chapter V, "Of the Superhuman Ideal," Ruskin explains, "It is evident that not only here is it unnecessary, but we are not altogether at liberty to trust for expression to the utmost ennobling of the human form; for we cannot do more than this, when that form is to be the actual representation, and not the recipient of Divine presence. Hence, in order to retain the actual humanity definitely we must leave upon it such signs of the operation of Sin and the liability to Death as are consistent with human ideality; and often more than these, definite signs of immediate and active evil . . ." (MP II, 316). In other words, for a human being to be represented truthfully as a human being, he or she must have signs of human imperfections. It follows that such signs cannot possibly be found on Christ's body since he is perfectly man, and, he is not merely the recipient of Divine presence, but indeed, represents the Divine presence in himself.[30] Without engaging

30. It may surprise readers to see how Ruskin even rejects the depictions of Christ by Fra Angelico—a painter he otherwise praises, elevating him above almost all other Renaissance painters. The passage I have in mind is also from chapter V, "Of the Superhuman Ideal." It runs, "I think this is almost self-evident, for it is clear that the illimitableness of Divine attributes cannot be by matter represented (though it may be typified); and I believe that all who are acquainted with the range of sacred art will admit, *not only that no representation of Christ has ever been even partially successful, but that the greatest painters fall therein below their accustomed level;* Perugino and Fra

in matters of personal taste, it can be pointed out that Ruskin's view here is perhaps unexpected, even unusual; it is not that he despises a realistic human form, because many of Fra Angelico's crucifixion frescoes are not realistic in Ruskin's art world of the nineteenth century but are highly idealized and poetic. Yet Ruskin will not accept the reality of Christ's bloody flesh in art. This does not fit into his system because, though it is truthful, it is not beautiful.

There is a further passage that reveals much about Ruskin's negative view of the flesh. This will be even more revealing when we acquaint ourselves with Pater's view of Hellenism toward the end of the volume and demonstrate how strongly Pater differs from Ruskin in his estimation of fleshly humanity. In contrasting the two orders of art, the ancient Greek ("pagan") on the one hand and the Italian Renaissance ("Christian") on the other, Ruskin argues, "Gather what we may of great, from Pagan chisel or Pagan dream, and set it beside the orderer of Christian warfare, Michael the Archangel [by Perugino] . . . no lines are there of earthly strength, no trace on the divine features of earthly anger; trustful, and thoughtful, fearless, but full of love, incapable except of the repose of eternal conquest, vessel and instrument of Omnipotence . . ." (MP II, 330). This eloquent passage continues, and before too long Ruskin concludes, "It is vain to attempt to pursue the comparison; the two orders of art have in

---

Angelico especially: Leonardo has, I think, done best; but perhaps the beauty of the fragment left at Milan . . . is as much dependent on the very untraceableness [*sic*] resulting from injury as on its original perfection. Of more daring attempts at representation of Divinity we need not speak; only this is to be noted respecting them, that though by the ignorant Romanists many such efforts were made under the idea of actual representation . . . by the nobler among them I suppose they were intended, and by us at any rate they may always be received, as mere symbols, the noblest that could be employed, but as much symbols still as a triangle, or the Alpha and Omega, nor do I think that the most scrupulous amongst Christians ought to desire to exchange the power obtained by the use of this symbol in Michael Angelo's creation of Adam and Eve, for the effect which would be produced by the substitution of any other sign in place of it." Ruskin, *MP* II, 317–18 (italics are mine). Ruskin seems to imply that attempts at making an "actual representation" of Christ almost always result in artistic failures. Real attempts at painting God (as Creator, etc.) will always be symbolic, not representational. This raises deeper theological issues about the very *possibility* of depicting Christ in art. If *no* attempts have even been even "*partially successful*," then what does Ruskin believe about the entire project throughout history? We have very little reflection from Ruskin on Orthodox Christ iconography as ancient and Byzantine icons were not yet widely known or reproduced in books in the West. Suffice it to say, Ruskin had less than charitable things to say about virtually every Renaissance depiction of Christ, except for one such as Da Vinci's, which remains a suggestive fragment.

them nothing common" (MP II, 331). This follows his extended discussion of the ways that the supernatural is manifested in history. So, Ruskin draws a complete contrast between pagan and Christian depictions of humanity in art, and argues that any signs of "earthly strength," such as we see in the best of Greek art, is vastly inferior to the more immaterial, heavenly forms of humanity that the Italian Renaissance artists gave to their men and angels. Ruskin further condemns the Greek trend toward physicality when he writes, "No herculean form is spiritual, for it is degrading the spiritual creature to suppose it operative through impulse of bone and sinew; its power is immaterial and constant, neither dependent on, nor developed by, exertion" (MP II, 327). Christian painters such as Michelangelo and Raphael stooped too low in depicting an earthy, fleshly ideal when they portrayed their men and women as muscular masses; Ruskin vilifies this style. He simply will have none of the physicality and sensuality of the human body that the ancient Greek art celebrates, that other later Renaissance masters glorify. He cannot find the Divine beauty he is looking for in the "bone and sinew" of the human body, in the blood of Christ's wounds, and generally in paintings that contain any hint of human sexuality. This is not surprising, however, because it is what we have seen throughout *Modern Painters*, Ruskin keeps physical flesh at arm's length and prefers to deal with non-human natural phenomena or, in the case of the Pisan and Venetian masters, medieval religious art when it avoids the Passion.[31]

In Ruskin's theoria, which is a *theological* aesthetic, Christ and Christ paintings have no real place. Even that classic subject of the crucifixion, found throughout all medieval and Renaissance schools of art, is either disappointing at best or abhorrent at worst. Ruskin simply has very little interest in Christ's flesh and no robust way of accounting for the paradox of a suffering Savior. When Christ is mentioned in *Modern*

31. Even when Ruskin does praise a particular form, such as Perugino's *Michael* which he declares to look like the "vessel and instrument of Omnipotence," he does not praise Perugino's *Michael* for those physical details that root him to this earth: details such as his very fine hair, floppy beret, or perfectly modeled late-medieval armor. Far from looking like a mere vessel for omnipotence; the angel could, in fact, be interpreted as a warrior who, fully armed, is ready to destroy God's enemies. My point is this: Ruskin is averse to the fleshiness of humanity in these artists, whether it is revealed in the suffering of Jesus or in the sinewy muscles of a fisherman-saint. He prefers the repose and perfection of the Divine attributes manifesting themselves throughout time. As we will see, Pater, Wilde, and Chesterton differ from Ruskin most strongly on this point.

Painters II, this is a Christ divorced from physical, fleshly reality. This is a heavenly Christ who stands beside the throne of his Father and not an earthly Christ condemned to suffer greatly and then die as a criminal. Christ is mentioned but certainly not highlighted in Ruskin's theology. The art critic seems to struggle to find a place for the Crucified One *aesthetically*.[32]

A few decades after the publication of *Modern Painters II*, the "art for art's sake" movement drew from the well of aesthetic insight and close observation while leaving behind what was, for Ruskin, the most important underlying concept of all beauty in art and the natural world: a God who is ever revealing himself. For example, Ruskin sets out the following necessary human responses for the right perception of beauty:

1. Sensual pleasure accompanied by joy.

2. Love of the object.

3. Perception of kindness of a superior intellect.

4. Veneration towards that intelligence itself. (MP II, 48)

These responses are a phenomenological approach to beauty; Ruskin wishes to demonstrate what happens to the great Italians, to Turner, and to himself in the presence of beauty, that is, what beauty *does* to all of them. Ruskin is not arguing that a critic must manufacture or cultivate these responses in herself or himself as part of some subjective force of will. These effects simply happen to those who are happy and pure in heart (MP II, 4). The "art for art's sake" movement will gladly accept the first two of the preceding points but not the third and fourth. As we will see, the aesthetes are primarily interested in this feeling, this *mood* that arises in the presence of beauty.

32. I reiterate that, as an Evangelical, Ruskin would not deny that Christ's death on the cross saved humanity from sin, but he struggles to situate any depictions of a suffering Christ—found throughout medieval and Renaissance paintings, of course—into his system, so focused as it was on truth, beauty, and morality.

2

Aesthesis

Walter Pater, Oscar Wilde, and Art for Art's Sake

IN THIS CHAPTER I will examine two major critical writings from the "art for art's sake" movement, coming from Walter Pater and his disciple Oscar Wilde. Pater and Wilde are not remembered today for being theologians or philosophers. However, it is far from the truth to think that Pater and Wilde avoided philosophical or theological questions. In their critical writings, these two eminent men of letters actually discuss religion a great deal; they frequently interpret artworks with Christian subject matter, often allude to the Christian Scriptures, demonstrate great learning in theological matters, and continually borrow religious vocabulary from spiritual writers and the church's liturgy. Most importantly, they show a great deal of interest in Jesus Christ and his teachings, though these teachings are often stripped of all the accumulated church dogmas from throughout history, thus leaving only the enigmatic sayings and the image of God incarnate, Jesus. Yet both Pater and Wilde found these teachings and this image to be exquisitely beautiful and forever influential. Pater and Wilde thus draw from the entire Christian experience, and they wrote to an audience that, unlike today, was still generally well versed in Christian matters. Pater and Wilde, in their call for an aesthetic criticism purified from any taint of metaphysics or morals, were influenced heavily by the German philosophical idealism that passed into Oxford, Cambridge, and educated circles through translators such as Coleridge.[1] In addition, these critics were heavily influence by

---

1. See my introduction.

48

literary figures that preceded them. I will briefly outline these influences before giving a careful reading of some key works demonstrating their "art for art's sake" aesthetic, which I will refer to throughout this chapter as aesthesis, that is, simple perception.

The American poet and theorist Edgar Allan Poe (1809–49) exerted a great and significant influence on most major French and British critics in the middle of the nineteenth century, including our two critics.[2] Poe's contribution to aesthetics is his insistence that poetry and all the arts must be "uncontaminated" by didacticism, history, morality, or belief.[3] His other major contribution is the idea that the artist produces work not through inspiration, but through careful and artificial construction designed to produce an emotional mood.[4] In a dated yet still highly valuable work on the history of aesthetics by Katharine Everett Gilbert, we read that, for Poe, "The artistic workman proceeds in the full light of his rational consciousness, closely watching and controlling every step. . . . As he starts on his work, the artist selects an effect which he wishes to produce, and his art consists in finding out and applying the proper means to this end."[5] Poe's theories on the separation of art from any moral or metaphysical foundation as well as his argument for the artificial crafting of artistic forms affected the views of all further writers and critics of the century, especially the aesthetes and decadents who followed him.

The French critic Theophile Gautier (1811–72), a sympathetic reader of Poe, shared many of his concerns. Gautier also had no patience for didacticism or utilitarianism in the arts; the arts must not teach because they should be useless:

> No, imbeciles, no, goitrous cretins that you are, a book does not make a gelatin soup; a novel is not a pair of seamless boots, a sonnet not a syringe throwing a continuous jet; a drama is not a rail-road—all essentially civilizing things which make humanity advance down the path of progress. By the bowels of all the popes past, present, and future, no and two hundred thousand times no![6]

2. Warner and Hough, *Strangeness and Beauty*, 2:145.

3. Warner and Hough, *Strangeness and Beauty*, 2:146.

4. Warner and Hough, *Strangeness and Beauty*, 2:147.

5. Everett Gilbert and Kuhn, *A History of Esthetics*, 494.

6. Warner and Hough, *Strangeness and Beauty*, 2:162.

In his concerns for the protection or even isolation of art from moral and metaphysical concerns, Gautier is another influence on and precursor to the two critics who influenced Chesterton's early views.

Charles Baudelaire (1821–67), through his supernaturalism and insistence on the power of symbols, is one of the most significant influences on the French *symbolistes* and is also influential for the aesthetes, Pater and Wilde, who would follow later in the century. For Baudelaire continued Poe's vision of the artist and Gautier's vision of the created product. He writes, "The artist owes nothing to anyone but himself. To future ages he holds out no promises but his own works. He is a guarantor of no one but himself. He died without offspring. He has been his own king, priest, and God."[7] There is this idea, coming to the fore in the mid-century through the Romantic critics, that the artist now fulfills the old roles that the priest once had, before the "disappearance of God." Baudelaire also further amplifies Gautier's point that art must never teach.

As critics, Pater and Wilde argue that the critical temperament is one especially attuned and ready to receive beautiful impressions as part of a spiritual yet also very earthy experience, one that is not concerned with moral philosophy or with traditional dogmas. Yet perhaps above all else, Pater and Wilde were also personally concerned with and fascinated by the beauty of Roman Catholicism. In Pater's only novel, the semi-autobiographical *Marius the Epicurean*, the protagonist converts to Roman Catholicism at the point of death after living an exquisite life of earthly pleasure.[8] Pater perhaps saw himself in such an artistic life with a beautiful deathbed conversion. Similarly, Oscar Wilde had a lifelong fascination with the Roman Church. His spiritual anguish and his curious deathbed reception into the Church years later are intriguing biographical details that I will cover in more detail below.

In this section I will conduct a close reading of Pater's most important critical work, *The Renaissance* (1873) and Wilde's major critical work, *Intentions* (1891); each is a collection of assorted essays dealing with various problems in aesthetics and including many interpretations of artworks. I will be comparing these works' views on the relation between beauty and morality, beauty and truth, and beauty and God, because I want to demonstrate not only both writers' debt to Ruskin, but also how these critics joined in a search for God, or at least a religion of beauty,

7. Warner and Hough, *Strangeness and Beauty*, 1:185.
8. See Pater, *Marius the Epicurean*.

that could withstand the critical pressures and honest doubts of the age. Pater and Wilde's search for this religion of beauty, if not inconclusive, is then certainly ambiguous. In worshiping the physicality of humanity, in yearning for something or someone beyond any system, they reach farther than Ruskin toward a more fleshly, incarnational theology, though it is one that can only be immanent, no matter how much it yearns for divinity and transcendence.

Walter Pater's *The Renaissance*

The art critic Peter Fuller described *The Renaissance* as "Ruskin inverted."[9] Everything that Ruskin set out to accomplish in *Modern Painters*—defend Turner as a kind of prophet, advance the purpose for artistic fidelity to nature, and reveal the moral-religious background of aesthetic perception—is turned upside down and inside out. However, Pater represents the next development of Ruskin's aesthetic in this age of "honest doubt" that I mentioned in the introduction: the search for a religious-like experience through purely immanent, earthly materiality. For Pater, the physicality of all beauty is not a *means* to a religious end; rather, the attainment of beauty *constitutes* a religious end in itself.

Because of the popularity and even *edginess* of this first collection of essays, Walter Pater became the "pioneering champion" of the "art for art's sake" movement.[10] In this celebrated work, *The Renaissance: Studies in Art and Poetry*, which is comprised of nine essays on art, Pater calls for a new movement in art criticism that would begin from the critic's own subjective perception and would interpret art apart from any didactic or moral meaning.[11] To usher in this new criticism, Pater wants this new type of critic to receive sensuous impressions from art and analyze such impressions of shapes, colors, tones, harmonies for the benefit of the public; such a critic will be one "[that] experiences these impressions strongly, and drives directly at the discrimination and analysis of them, has no need to trouble himself with the abstract question what beauty is in itself, or what its exact relation to truth or experience—metaphysical questions, as unprofitable as metaphysical questions elsewhere"

9. Fuller, *Theoria*, 119.

10. Fraser, *Beauty and Belief*, 197.

11. Pater, *The Renaissance: Studies in Art and Poetry*. Hereafter I will cite this work within this chapter as (*Renaissance*, page #).

(*Renaissance*, xvii). For Pater the critic must dabble in all matters of beauty and then has the task of making a discriminating analysis of his or her own aesthetic experience.[12] Such a critic may then present his or her aesthetic discoveries to the public for their benefit. The critic also has the task of showing the public the disunity between religion, morality, and beauty. In doing so he or she essentially follows a Kantian aesthetic with its emphasis on the non-relation between morality and the discernment of the beautiful.[13] Yet, this aesthetic is also far removed from Kant because of its unabashed devotion to materiality and sensuality. In this exercise the critic elevates the aesthetic experience itself above other human concerns, including morality or religion, turning such appreciation into a form of worship.

More specifically, I argue in this section that, like Ruskin, Pater regards the perception of beauty as a pleasurable event, but where Ruskin argues this pleasure is more of a spiritual and moral satisfaction, Pater most definitely has in mind physical, sensual satisfaction—though explained in spiritual and religious terms. While Ruskin could not accommodate the sexual, the fleshly, or the immoral in his aesthetic system, Pater certainly can. Though, in discarding God during his quest for this immanent and enfleshed religion of beauty, he fails to find anything except a continual desire that burns more and more. Pater is left with chasing after exquisite moments ever desiring more and more beauty.

Beauty & Morality in *The Renaissance*

In this major work, Pater is hardly concerned with social morals or personal conduct, and he declines to discuss any other past theory regarding the relationship of ethics to aesthetics. Indeed, the question of moral meaning and didactic potential in art is discarded along with all those broader "metaphysical questions," questions that are, as a whole, totally unprofitable to the matter of aesthetics (*Renaissance*, xvii). Art has no other purpose, no outside message to communicate to the viewer; rather,

12. Pater sees the critic as a kind of *sommelier* of beauty, that is, an expert who sees, smells, tastes, recommends, directs, and passes along beautiful things without ever going into metaphysics, ethics, or religion.

13. Kant writes in his *Critique of Judgment*, ¶42, "Now I willingly admit that the interest in the beautiful of art . . . gives no evidence at all of a habit of mind attached to the morally good, or even inclined that way." Quoted in Simpson, *German Aesthetic and Literary Criticism*, 58.

the delightful lines, colors, shapes, and shadows form the very purpose itself. The meaning is all there on the surface, not dwelling below as an eternal idea or dwelling above as immaterial spirit. Pater writes very revealingly, "[A] great picture has no more definite message for us than an accidental play of sunlight and shadow for a few moments on the wall or floor . . ." (*Renaissance*, 133). A beautiful work does not carry a message that can morally improve a human being; it does not have a moving lesson to inspire anyone to feelings of faith or to acts of charity. A painting, even a great painting, will be just like the sunlight and shadow that accidentally play in one's room, teaching nothing, imparting nothing, and communicating nothing. Rather, in and of itself, it simply dazzles and delights. The goal of any work of art is to give an impression of "untranslatable charm" to its viewer for his or her own pleasure (*Renaissance*, 133). Any piece of art that supposedly was painted to teach the viewer some lesson becomes a didactic tool and ceases to be a piece with any artistic merit.

Therefore, for Pater, the beautiful impression received from an artwork is what matters and never morals or metaphysical questions. To become embroiled in matters of religion or metaphysics is to miss the point of art. Gone is the Ruskinian insistence on a pure heart, pure taste, pure imagination. In Pater the only "purity," if he were even to use such a word, is the bright reflection or charm in the work of art itself.

Yet, in arguing against the moral center of aesthetics, Pater is not arguing for an increase of debauchery in the world or for all artists to have an excuse for licentiousness. He has no anti-morality agenda. In his discussion of Peter Abelard and medieval French dramatists (as kinds of proto-Renaissance aesthetes), his concern is to show that Christian dogmas bind and prevent the "blossoming of the humanist ideal," not that they are bad in an ethical sense; the problem is therefore not Christ, who actually was a humanist because of his concern for humans, but dogmas people have concocted about him (*Renaissance*, 24). The love of beauty, the worship of the body, the study of material things are beyond religious-ethical rules (*Renaissance*, 24). In writing that aesthetic appreciation is beyond dogmas or rules, Pater is not declaring aesthetics to be contrary to religion, but rather contrary to a certain narrow religiosity that would devalue the physical.

Is Pater too far from Ruskin's theoria? In certain respects, no. Pater's examples of heroic aesthetes are not just any famous people; they are the greatest lovers, artists, and critics of the world—women and men who were perfectly attuned to the beauty of the cosmos. Their conception of art (like Pater's, of course) has nothing to do with human intelligence, for art is always striving "to be independent of the mere intelligence" and to "present one single effect to the 'imaginative reason,' that complex faculty for which every thought and feeling is twin-born with its sensible analogue or symbol" (*Renaissance*, 138). Ruskin's theoria was also above human intelligence or mere emotions (MP II, 42); the theoretic act is a contemplative act of the heart, mind, and body in unison. Beauty is not so much understood in the head as it is experienced in the depths of the a beholder's soul.

In Pater's remarks on the "complex faculty,"[14] he also anticipates a later Chestertonian idea: that those artistic, sensible analogues—the different colors on an artist's canvas or notes on a composer's score—inexplicably and mysteriously correspond to movements of the inner life. Chesterton's notion of the "reality behind symbols" that he develops in his book *G. F. Watts* (1904) during an interpretation of the painting called "Hope" is his realization that all paintings, like all words, are attempts by human beings to catch a "broken instantaneous glimpse" of that which is even a "mystery to saints."[15] More on this book later.

For now, we also need to note that Pater does make the comparison between the best of pictorial art and music (*Renaissance*, 139). This was certainly not foreign to Ruskin, who was Pater's teacher, precursor, and influence, but this type of language tends to be more consistent in Ruskin, who subordinates everything according to its ability to communicate God's truth. In Ruskin there is a sort of hierarchy of artistic types, which is not picked up by Pater. Here the critic asserts that each art, from painting to sculpture to music, has its own "peculiar and untranslatable, sensuous charm," and that these arts are *not* different languages that seek to express the one, same truth (*Renaissance*, 130). Yet Pater still insists that in the visual arts, the aim is to so completely blend the means and the ends that particular art works become more like music (*Renaissance*, 139). So, Pater affirms that music's charm is different from painting's charm, in other words, both music and painting have their unique form, but the best kind of painting is that which is most like music.

There seems to be a contradiction here, for if all arts have their own untranslatable charm, then painting's charm should not strive to be more

14. A phrase that Pater invents and does not adequately explain or defend. He almost sounds similar to the French *symbolistes* in this passage.

15. Chesterton, *G. F. Watts*, 97.

like music's charm. After all, in Pater's view, neither has a message—moral or otherwise—to convey. Yet Pater concludes that the chief aesthetic ideal of music is its contentlessness. Is he therefore implying that pictorial art cannot help but contain some kind of content or deliver some kind of message? And that as art becomes "better" or "purer" it sheds off this content to become more music-like? Perhaps here Pater is knowingly or not following one of his great philosophical influences, Hegel, in his belief that the arts must be ranked by their ability to communicate spirit. Hegel writes about this belief that poetry is the highest Art because, "[I]t expresses directly for its own apprehension the spirit with all its imaginative and artistic conceptions but without setting these visibly and bodily for contemplation from the outside."[16] Poetry thus gives the essence of the spirit in the most direct, pointed fashion. Perhaps Pater's previous words on the "complex faculty" could provide further help here; if every type of human emotion has a corresponding symbol, it may be that poetry is the broadest means of symbolizing and thus triggering these emotions. In any case, Pater sees the arts, especially poetry, as stirring within the beholder specific feelings that are untranslatable, but that direct the beholder to the art-object itself again and again. In this art-object may be "spirit" of some sort, but Pater would define it as simply the essence of beauty. It is not something to gain, but to gaze upon.

Beauty & Truth in *The Renaissance*

Walter Pater frequently uses the word *charm* in his essays (*Renaissance*, 19, 72, etc.). By using this word he is saying that there is nothing beyond or beneath the beautiful surface of the piece of art itself. Like a musical composition with its rhythm, melodies, and harmonies, the physical painting or sculpture has its lines, colors, and textures, but these are not signifiers for deeper truths. Rather, the truth of art lies in the purest beauty that is displayed by the artist and received by the discerning critic. This is not some kind of inner, metaphysical beauty that leads one to attain higher, invisible truth; rather, it is simply a beauty existing on the outside. The discerning critic must receive the surface-level beauty of a painting, of a statue, of a piece of music. This surface is all that matters. Interpreting Renaissance artists like Giorgione and Titian, Pater argues that these Venetian artists realized the "truth" that painting "must be

16. Simpson, *German Aesthetic and Literary Criticism*, 233.

before all things decorative" (*Renaissance*, 140). Pater's use of the word "truth" here should not go unnoticed. Such decorative beauty does not uncover objective truth; neither does it interpret truth, unveil truth, or communicate truth. Rather, beauty *is* truth, the highest mode of expression that exists, and such beauty is experienced, analyzed, interpreted when it is properly received by an art critic.[17] Pater thus holds one of the "false opinions" that Ruskin critiques in *Modern Painters II* in that he holds that truth *is* beauty.

Throughout these essays Pater also stresses the subjectivity inherent in both creation and in aesthesis. He urges his reader to ask the question, "What is this song or picture, this engaging personality presented in life or in a book, to *me*? What effect does it really produce on me?" (*Renaissance*, xviii). Shortly after this he argues that the art critic should not bother with definitions of beauty, but must attain "a certain kind of temperament, the power of being deeply moved by the presence of beautiful objects" (*Renaissance*, xx). One's own unique perception is a precious experience and constitutes a very true experience to the beholder. This is an inner, subjective ability to be cultivated and given its due attention.

In his famous conclusion to *The Renaissance*, Pater writes, "Of such wisdom, the poetic passion, the desire for beauty, the love of art for its own sake, has most [importance]. For art comes to you proposing frankly to give nothing but the highest quality to your moments as they pass, and simply for those moments' sake" (*Renaissance*, 239). Since beauty has no higher function than to physically and emotionally delight by its sheer *charm*, there is no need for a complex definition. The truth of beauty lies in its experience, what it gives to the beholder by means of its decorative charm and aesthetic delight. Pater writes,

> With this sense of the splendour of our experience and of its awful brevity, gathering all we are into one desperate effort to see and touch, we shall hardly have time to make theories about the things we see and touch. What we have to do is to be forever curiously testing new opinions and courting new impressions, never acquiescing in a facile orthodoxy of Comte, or of Hegel, or of our own. Philosophical theories or ideas, as points of view, instruments of criticism, may help us to gather up what might otherwise pass unregarded by us. "Philosophy is the microscope of thought." The theory or idea or system which requires of us the sacrifice of any part of this experience, in consideration

17. Ruskin, of course, would vociferously disagree! See MP II, 64.

of some interest into which we cannot enter, or some abstract
theory we have not identified with ourselves. . . .[18]

This "facile orthodoxy" is the common enemy of not only Pater and
the aesthetes, but of Ruskin. Once again here is evidence of Pater's debt
to Ruskin. For both hold that in any shallow system, indirect discussion
replaces direct experience, and complicated rules theoretically explained
detract from simple truths directly experienced. Ruskin argues in *Modern Painters* for a simple and intuitive approach to beauty (and then
ultimately, to the knowledge of God the Father). This direct, aesthetic
perception is all that Pater asks his readers to practice as well, for in aesthesis one already enjoys the whole meaning of life with its myriad forms,
colors, textures, and beauties. Pater would argue that if a person could
simply experience it and not waste any effort forming theories about it,
then she or he would fully enjoy these splendid, passionate moments as
life itself. Three final conclusions are worth pointing out regarding Pater's
view of truth in aesthetics.

The first is that Pater believes in truth. His question is not Pilate's
question, "What is truth?" For Pater truth certainly exists, but in some
inexplicable and mysterious way *truth is beauty* to be discovered not
through the intellect but through the eyes and heart. Beautiful truth in
its complexity and brilliance is revealed at certain points in the history of
the breaking forth of the human spirit, such as the Renaissance. It is not
so much dissected through theory as it is experienced directly through
aesthesis at the highest moments of spiritual contemplation. The very fact
that Pater uses this language about the emergence of the human spirit
at different points in human history is a hint of the influence of Hegel,
though not of Hegel's entire system.

The second conclusion is that truth must be discovered through
experimentation, that is, through many and various experiences. Pater is
not a nihilist, for he does not declare that this continual seeking is impossible, vain, or meaningless. On the contrary, truth is only found when it
breaks forth at certain special moments and the human beholder (critic)
is ready to selflessly accept it. In passionately seeking after those moments, artist-lovers from Peter Abelard to Pater himself have experienced
the truth that breaks forth in beauty.

Thirdly, the only type of truth that Pater will accept is that which
one might *enter*. Philosophy may be the microscope of thought, but Pater

18. Pater, *The Renaissance*, 237.

is ready to cast it aside if it leads away from his direct experiences. Abstract theories may be important in a way, but only insofar as they enlarge the truths already there to be discovered in visions of rapturous beauty.

Beauty & God in *The Renaissance*

How to explain the purpose of life is one of the central problems in Pater's *The Renaissance*. The ultimate message Pater has for the reader is that every individual's total experience of life, with its passions and beauties, is an "interlude" before death, made up of priceless moments that must be completely experienced in order to give one's pitifully short life any meaning (*Renaissance*, 238). Human life is thus defined by the powerful aesthetic encounters it has with the outbreaking spirit of beauty.

In lieu of any traditional, theological conception of eternal or immortal life for human beings, Pater offers his idea of the aesthetically experienced moment that approaches eternity but can only exist in this world. Such a moment, which feels longer than it actually is, functions as the only possible channel for reprieve, peace, and joy in the midst of a very short and very imperfect life. Pater writes,

> To such a tremulous wisp constantly re-forming itself on the stream, to a single sharp impression, with a sense in it, a relic more or less fleeting, of such moments gone by, what is real in our life fines itself down. It is with this movement, with the passage and dissolution of impressions, images, sensations, that analysis leaves off—that continual vanishing away, that strange, perpetual weaving and unweaving of ourselves.[19]

This is a tenuous conception of the very temporary experience of a (beautiful) moment. For the sad fate of humankind is to always lose the sensation as soon as it is attained, to become "unweaved," as Pater puts it, even after one is "weaved" by whatever exquisite experience one had. There is a tragedy in the slipping away of time and the unraveling of all experience. Pater responds with a pointed question a few lines later when he asks, "How shall we pass most swiftly from point to point, and be present always at the focus where the greatest number of vital forces unite in their purest energy?" (*Renaissance*, 236). This swift passage is the goal of life.

Yet is it even possible to be "present always" at the point where beautiful, charming experiences flow together, uniting in such a way? Pater

19. Pater, *The Renaissance*, 236.

answers with the words, "To burn always with this hard, gemlike flame, to maintain this ecstasy, is success in life" (*Renaissance*, 236). Such a burning often looks like desperate grasping, for exquisite shapes, colors, and textures are not always readily available (*Renaissance*, 237). But this grasping must continue; indeed, human beings must do all they can to desperately grasp, again and again, for those sensory experiences are all that human beings have. Is anyone able to do this over and over again, though?

In a mellifluous and poetical prose passage on the *Mona Lisa*, Pater writes that Da Vinci has somehow captured the possibility in "Lady Lisa's" expression, this kind of cyclical, perpetual enjoyment of various experiences: "The fancy of a perpetual life, sweeping together ten thousand experiences, is an old one; and modern philosophy has conceived the idea of humanity as wrought upon by, and summing up in itself, all modes of thought and life. Certainly Lady Lisa might stand as the embodiment of the old fancy, the symbol of the modern idea" (*Renaissance*, 126). In this work by the great Renaissance genius, a thousand passions from a thousand years have been preserved—captured—in a perfectly timeless repose. Pater treats the Lady Lisa in almost a religiously typological way; her sensuous charm is in no way devalued, but it points forward to a higher reality in which all aesthetic expression is gathered: the modern idea. The modern idea, that "cyclical enjoyment of various experiences," makes room to include all forms of beautiful tradition, ritual, and history, when they guide the viewer to moments of ecstasy. Any of these perpetual modes of enjoyment can include Christian expressions if they are beautiful and expressive.

Pater does not, therefore, cavalierly dismiss religion, faith, or spirituality in *The Renaissance*. Yet in these collected essays Pater takes a skeptical and generally negative view toward "Christendom" as such. He insists on the fact that organized, authoritarian religion has only ever prevented the blossoming of art (*Renaissance*, 24) and that traditional Christianity in general has devalued the flesh and enslaved the spirit (*Renaissance*, 184). In this separation of art and religion, Pater attempts to preserve beauty from what he sees as the corrupting influence of doctrine, and distances his aestheticism from any ideal that could possibly bind or limit this ideal perception of beauty (*Renaissance*, 24). Pater interprets the Renaissance as a critical moment in the history of the human spirit, when there was that outbreaking of the free spirit and a celebration of humanism, "in which the love of the things of the intellect and the imagination for their own sake" became greater than the love of intellectual or imaginative things that existed for the sake of bolstering moral philosophy or supporting the Christian church (*Renaissance*, 2).

Yet in this work Pater adopts (or adapts) religious language in his discussion of the critic's aesthetic experience. Sense-impressions may be devoid of outside moral, religious, or philosophical content, but in themselves these impressions form the raw material for a new religion of aesthesis. Pater intentionally calls for a new movement in aesthetics that re-appropriates traditional religious experiences and vocabulary, and this movement—which loves, worships, and sacrifices to beauty—takes on ritualistic, spiritual, mystical, and even monastic dimensions. Pater's famous final words in *The Renaissance* demonstrate this.[20]

It is therefore interesting that Pater begins this work that would become the sacred text of the "art for art's sake" movement by musing upon the mediaeval scholastic theologian Peter Abelard. In Pater's interpretation, Abelard was an ecclesiastical outsider, probing deeper than the established orthodoxy allowed, who was also wrongly rejected and misunderstood by the religious authorities of the day. In Abelard Pater sees a twelfth-century aesthete, a hero and forerunner of the Renaissance humanist, and also, perhaps, a spiritual-aesthetic forerunner of this critic himself. In Abelard's passion for Heloise and his yearning for beautiful love, he is an example of someone who tragically lived the "art for art's sake" ideal; Pater writes that in Abelard "we see . . . that [aesthetic] spirit going abroad, . . . its intimacy, its languid sweetness, its rebellion, its subtle skill in dividing the elements of human passion, its care for physical beauty, its worship of the body . . ." (*Renaissance*, 5). Abelard's aesthetic spirit, his impassioned love for Heloise and for the delights of physical pleasure, did not replace his Christianity but in a sense transcended it. Abelard is thus a perfect example of that type of critic whom Pater praises, one who neither worships dusty dogmas nor enslaves him- or herself to a rigid system of morals, but instead receives those sensations, pleasures, and passions that are the pinnacle of human life. These exquisite impressions are opposed to traditional religion with its canon laws and regulations, its devaluing of the body and insecurity with sexuality. So, this medieval theologian "prefigures the character of the Renaissance, that movement in which, in various ways, the human mind wins for itself a new kingdom of feeling, and sensation and thought, not opposed to

20. As do Wilde's final words in "The Critic as Artist," which I introduce later in this chapter.

but only beyond and independent of the spiritual system then actually realised" (*Renaissance*, 6).

Abelard is thus one of the boldest critics in his assertions that there is something beautiful about sexual love and the human body, something about such beauties that drive a person to the act of worship. Pater says this point of view is "not opposed to but beyond and independent of the spiritual system" (*Renaissance*, 6). These words are significant. These impressions of beauty—physical, sexual, material—are far greater and, if received and enjoyed correctly, they actually open up a point of view that lies "beyond" all religious dogma (*Renaissance*, 24). In Pater's glorifying of the perfection of the human body, he is rebelling against those (perceived) theological and philosophical currents that devalued physical bodies. Pater longs for an established and embodied religion of beauty.

Similarly, in his discussion of Greek art, Pater admires any work, such as the *Venus of Melos*, that glorifies the human body; he writes that this work exemplifies "[t]he mind [that] begins and ends with the finite image, yet loses no part of the spiritual motive" (*Renaissance*, 205). His argument is that the Greeks who carved the *Venus* and the other statues that seem to glory in every curve of the human body had a spiritual motive that was more spiritual, not less spiritual, for this bodily worship. Warner and Hough note that Pater's writing is marked by this "natural supernaturalism,"[21] that for him spirit and substance are inseparable in the work of art. This inseparability makes the physical statue of the Greeks praiseworthy. Similarly, Paterian scholar Kate Hext writes that, for Pater, "Venus suggests not the eradication of spirit with sensuality, but rather a pantheistic fusion of spirit and matter."[22] When Hext uses the word "pantheistic" here, she does not mean in a strict sense that Pater believed God or "the gods" were to be found in all of nature. Rather, she points to his urge to modify this "dichotomy between the sensual and the spiritual," a dichotomy that is pervasive, no doubt, in post-Kantian Victorian culture.[23]

Pater then sees that the Greeks had a spiritual motive that was not lessened by its fixation on the surface of the body but was deepened by it. The experience of beauty in the minds of the sculptors and in the hearts of the viewers has nothing to do with theoretical religious tenets from their

21. Warner and Hough, *Strangeness and Beauty*, 2:5.

22. Hext, *Walter Pater: Individualism and Aesthetic Philosophy*, 95.

23. Hext, *Walter Pater: Individualism and Aesthetic Philosophy*, 94–95.

philosophical and religious beliefs but rather stemmed from a deeper, more primitive sensuality that nevertheless lost nothing of spiritual motives. Pater's remarks on Greek sculpture are clearly opposed to Ruskin's views, already encountered, in *Modern Painters II.*

In this estimation of the sensuous surfaces of Greek art, Pater's "spiritual motive" is undeniably present; he sees art for art's sake as the way to cut through the burdens of dogma and ethics and so to expose the flaming center of human life, which certain artists and poets have laid bare throughout the highest moments of history. This is the experience of spirit and matter in one complete, sensuous whole.

This enjoyment of spirit and matter melded together is not overtly Christian in Pater. It is certainly not an explicit "theology of the body" or "sacramental theology" in the strictest sense. However, we can detect the echoes of such a theological striving in his aesthetics. Pater declares that life's purpose is to burn; "To burn always with this hard, gemlike flame, to maintain this ecstasy, is success in life" (*Renaissance*, 236). This notable and powerful sentence demonstrates that the critic's purpose in life is not to find salvation or eventually reach heaven; it is to "burn" with pleasurable sense-perceptions, to take in as much bodily, physical charm as possible before expiring.

Pater continually fashions his aesthetic essays utilizing spiritual imagery, religious language, and biblical allusion. In the final paragraph of his work Pater seems to reference words from the Apostle Paul's second letter to the Corinthians about a "sentence of death," and he also references Christ's words as recorded in Luke's parable of the unjust steward, about "the sons [children] of the world."[24] In an interesting yet brief allusion to these scriptural passages, Pater writes:

> [For] we are all under sentence of death but with a sort of indefinite reprieve . . . : we have an interval, and then our place knows us no more. Some spend this interval in listlessness, some in high passions, the wisest, at least among "the children of the world," in art and song. For our one chance lies in expanding that interval, in getting as many pulsations as possible into the given time. Great passions may give us this quickened sense of

24. The "sentence of death" is a reference to 2 Corinthians 1:9: "Indeed, we felt that we had received the sentence of death. But that was to make us rely not on ourselves but on God who raises the dead." The "children of the world" is a reference to Luke 16:8: "The master commended the dishonest manager for his shrewdness. For the sons of this world are more shrewd in dealing with their own generation than the sons of light."

life, ecstasy and sorrow of love, the various forms of enthusias-
tic activity, disinterested or otherwise, which come naturally to
many of us. Only be sure it is passion—that it does yield you this
fruit of a quickened, multiplied consciousness.[25]

Whereas in Saint Paul's letter, this language about the "sentence of death"
was intended to convince the Corinthians to trust in God who has power
over such death, Pater makes a much more pessimistic point. This "sentence of death" is fate; there is the interval of life, and then all experiences
simply cease. One must therefore be sure to hold onto those experiences
of beauty. Aesthesis is religion, for it provides meaning to the purpose of
life and even ritual for accomplishing its ends; its "texts" are the paintings
of Giorgione and Leonardo, and the writings of Abelard and Winckel-
mann. Anything that gives this passion, including the words of the New
Testament, may be used by the aesthete to bring forth fruit from "a quickened, multiplied consciousness" (*Renaissance*, 238).

Pater then freely borrows Christ's language about "the children
of the world," but he gives these children a radically different task than
Jesus of Nazareth does. Rather than calling for them to be cunning in
their relations with others by generosity, love, and compassion, they are
to be wise in art and song. Pater's usage of the New Testament here is
subtle, yet important. This is one more section of *The Renaissance* where
he redefines aesthetic enjoyment as a kind of new consciousness in the
history of mankind, a consciousness giving rise to a new understanding
to all human striving, including all religions. Pater's art for art's sake view
does not reject all Christian things; rather, the Christian tradition and the
person of Christ himself can be interpreted and even enjoyed in a new,
aesthetic sense.

Final Reflections on Pater

Walter Pater reaches several stunning conclusions on beauty's relation
to morality, truth, and religion. We have seen that Pater believes morality has little to do with enjoying life's exquisite moments, but actually
detracts from them. Morality must be separate from the enjoyment of
beauty, though morality and beauty are not directly opposed to one another. We've also seen that in Pater's view, beauty is a subjective response
of the receiver, and the artistic truth of color, line, form is the only truth

25. Pater, *The Renaissance*, 238.

to be concerned with. This is an earthy and physical truth that breaks out in different epochs. Then also conventional religion should be valued by the type of aesthetic experience it produces, though the study of aesthetic experience creates a new kind of consciousness that can fill the void left by the absence of religion in a skeptical age. Pater argues that the conventional mysticism and monasticism of Christians throughout the ages has served only to devalue the glories of the body and human creativity. This is most certainly because such passions and visions were seen as means to ends rather than the highest, most beautiful experiences themselves. For Pater, what is now needed is an unorthodox religion of beauty, a humanist aesthetic where the critics serve as priests and beauty is the only dogma. It is the task of the critics, the task of Pater, to demonstrate that beautiful things are to be worshiped for their own sake.

Pater strives to demonstrate that receiving beauty is an experience beyond religious dogmas, but not exactly above religious feeling. For Pater freely uses Christian language; he dwells at length on religious thinkers and artists; and all the time he is concerned with how women and men find meaning in their lives. Pater stays far away from the kind of critical analysis of Christianity that figures like Strauss, Renan, and Arnold engaged in, but he is certainly responding to the general religious feelings and doubts of the century. It is therefore interesting that he strives after an ideal apprehension where the aesthete can soak in beauty, experiencing it as truth beyond any dogma and deeper than any confession. Beauty, like the Catholicism Pater so appreciated, simply *is*, and it demands to be enjoyed for its own sake.

Oscar Wilde's *Intentions*

Oscar Wilde, who came to know and deeply respect both Pater and Ruskin while at Oxford in the 1870s, came to regard *The Renaissance* as his "golden book" that shaped his views toward art and life.[26] Yet by the time of the publication of his 1891 work, *Intentions*, Wilde had come into his own as spokesman for the "art for art's sake" movement. *Intentions* forms the middle work in Wilde's three books of criticism he was to publish in his lifetime.[27] Like Pater's *The Renaissance*, this is also a compila-

26. Fraser, *Beauty and Belief: Aesthetics and Religion in Victorian Literature*, 187.

27. The other two being *Historical Criticism* (1879), and *The Soul of Man* (1891). See Guy, *The Complete Works of Oscar Wilde*, vol. 4. Contained in this volume is Wilde's *Intentions*. Hereafter I cite the work edited by Guy parenthetically as (*Intentions*, page #).

tion of essays originally published separately: "The Decay of Lying," "Pen, Pencil, and Poison," "The Critic as Artist," and "The Truth of Masks." In these works, Wilde more frequently means poetry, literature, and drama when he uses the word "art," yet he is also promoting an aesthetic view that takes on a more broadly inclusive definition of art as any beautiful human activity that is done for its own sake. It is Wilde's first and third essays in this work that most clearly set up his "art for art's sake" position. They are deliciously satirical and irreverent, written with stylistic flair and a strong use of paradox. It is not my goal to connect *Intentions* to the rest of Wilde's writings nor to situate it within the wider sexual, social, and political critiques during the *fin de siècle*. Scholars such as Lawrence Danson have already done just this.[28] I simply want to uncover what Wilde says about art and how he thinks beauty relates to theology and religious experience.

"The Decay of Lying" is a dialogue between Vivian, a dandy who acts as a spokesman for the aesthetic movement, and Cyril, his patient and attentive friend. Cyril approaches Vivian who is reading inside a private library and tries to invite him only to "go and lie on the grass, and smoke cigarettes, and enjoy nature," but Vivian responds harshly, criticizing nature itself and explaining to his friend why art is so superior to it (*Intentions*, 73). As their conversation about this unfolds, Vivian tells Cyril of an article he is penning called "The Decay of Lying: A Protest" (*Intentions*, 74). Vivian then proceeds to read aloud this article, though he interrupts himself frequently. Wilde's intention in "The Decay of Lying" is to show that art is actually a lie, and the artist, a liar. But lies are interesting and liars are delightful, so says Vivian, whereas nature (and "real" life) is boring. As we know after reviewing Ruskin's *Modern Painters*, such a view of nature could not be farther from Ruskin's overtly theological aesthetic. Wilde is unconcerned with the Romantic notion of nature's power to move others to worship and praise. Nature is something in the way of people's artistic progress because it "keeps on repeating [its] effect until we all become absolutely wearied of it" (*Intentions*, 95). Wilde, via his character Vivian, criticizes nature along with life, which he also considers to be overwhelmingly boring. From the outset of this dialogue Vivian is sarcastic, witty, and intentionally paradoxical.

The second essay ("Pen, Pencil, and Poison") concerns the style of a much-forgotten figure from earlier in the century: the poisoner Thomas

---

28. See Danson, *Wilde's Intentions: The Artist in His Criticism.*

Griffiths Wainewright. Though this article is briefer than the other three in *Intentions*, Wilde still has adequate space to develop his critical and aesthetic ideas based around the "art for art's sake" creed.

The third essay in *Intentions*, "The Critic as Artist," is also in the form of a dialogue, this time between a bitingly brilliant critic named Gilbert and an antagonist named Ernest who is converted from his previous traditional aesthetic views by Gilbert's "absurdly sophistical argument" that critics are, in fact, more creative than artists (*Intentions*, 154, 187). As this dialogue develops, Wilde has Gilbert develop more paradoxes, including the idea that by only by leaving religion behind can a person become divine.

The final essay, "The Truth of Masks," is a piece on Shakespeare and his costumes, and it turns into another exploration of contradiction in art. The essence of art is contradiction, and Shakespeare's use of costumes to hide the truth actually discloses it, in an aesthetic way.

Overall Wilde's essays are more eclectic than Pater's in *The Renaissance*. Whereas Pater's function like chapters in a book somewhat loosely centered around a common theme, Wilde's are less connected, with two of the essays being imaginative dialogues. Yet, the four essays in *Intentions* all loudly sound forth the call of art for art's sake. As we approach these important essays, we must ask how does Wilde respond to the issues of morality, truth, and God in his *Intentions*, and what does this response owe to the influence of both Ruskin and Pater? Like the previous section on Pater, I will examine how Wilde's aesthetic addresses the religious situation at the end of the nineteenth century, and how his aesthetic approach also represents another Victorian pathway through the loss-of-faith narrative. Wilde rejects the God-centered, yet bodiless, religion of beauty found in his Oxford professor, John Ruskin, though he undoubtedly owes much to the art critic's influence. Then he joins with Pater in the cry of "art for art's sake," sharing Pater's passion for the physicality of humanity, yet also his urge for something resembling religious belonging and transcendence. I will demonstrate through my close reading that Wilde utilizes biblical allusions, religious feeling, and mystical terminology in an endeavor to find a replacement for the Christian faith, which seemed to be more difficult to accept in the nineteenth century than ever before. Yet Wilde is even more of an enigma than Pater for at least two reasons: his ever-present (and self-described) antinomianism and his lifelong obsession with Catholicism, which is apparent in this collection.

Beauty & Morality in *Intentions*

In "The Decay of Lying" we hear from Vivian that "Art, very fortunately, has never once told us the truth," an intentionally shocking line that naturally stands opposed to virtually everything Ruskin ever wrote (*Intentions*, 99). This is to say that art should be unconcerned with anything so uninteresting and dogmatic as the moral duty of communicating truth. It instead has the higher duty of expressing only itself (*Intentions*, 96). Wilde will have nothing to do with the puritanical preaching of rules and ordinances.[29]

On the infamous poisoner Thomas Griffiths Wainewright, Wilde writes, "There is no essential incongruity between crime and culture. We cannot re-write the whole course of history for the purpose of gratifying our moral sense of what it should be" (*Intentions*, 121). Then, after pointing out that infamous figures such as Nero, Tiberius, and Caesar Borgia have become more like "puppets in a play" than like real personages, to judge from a perceived higher moral ground, Wilde writes, "They have passed into the sphere of art and science, and neither art nor science knows anything of moral approval or disapproval" (*Intentions*, 121). Art, like science, is by definition set apart from ethics; neither sensations nor cold, hard facts can have moralizing effects. They simply present the facts of physical perception and history.

In "The Critic as Artist" we find some of Wilde's boldest, wildest statements about the division between art and morality. Ernest declares, "All art is immoral" (*Intentions*, 174), and later clarifies with the phrase, "Aesthetics are higher than ethics. They belong to a more spiritual sphere. To discern the beauty of a thing is the finest point to which we can arrive" (*Intentions*, 204). Following moral rules is not a spiritual task, yet the contemplation of the beauty of a thing is something deeply spiritual. Not only is Wilde totally unconcerned with moral issues, rules, and laws, but he openly declares, "The artistic critic, like the mystic, is an antinomian always" (*Intentions*, 204). This means that for the critic of art, the contemplative individual who is especially attuned to matters of exquisite beauty, the law of God and the law of nature are, quite simply, *never* a concern. Any law with its ethical demands belongs to the lower realm of action,

---

29. It is important to note that Wilde has in mind all the arts when he uses the term "art," though he readily admits that literature is a more perfect form of art than painting. In any case, Wilde's opinion that art cannot teach or tell the truth stands opposed, at least at first sight, to Ruskin's insistence that art is primarily a means of communicating the truth of nature, and thus, the truth of God.

which belongs to that boring world of real life, not of contemplation. With Wilde's insistence on contemplation, the story of Mary and Martha as told in the Gospel of Luke might come to mind.[30]

The aim of art is never to move a person to action, but to create a mood. As the mystics do not worry about laws, according to Wilde, so neither does the critic worry herself or himself about them, either.[31] The critic must only seek the proper mood, and the attainment of this mood has significant similarities to the Christian contemplative tradition. Wilde mentions that while this mood-creation is highly unpractical, it is necessary (*Intentions*, 179). We will consider this word "mood" in the later section on "Beauty & God in *Intentions*," but for now, to sum up this position on the relation between beauty and morality, Wilde's character says, "The critic should be able to recognise that the sphere of Art and the sphere of Ethics are absolutely distinct and separate. When they are confused, Chaos has come again" (*Intentions*, 189).

In this division of aesthetics and ethics Wilde is arguing for the integrity of art; if it were to become a tool to something else, whether that is personal or corporate ethical action, its own value as a beautiful artefact would be attenuated. The idea that art, to be truly art, must exist for its own sake and not as a prop or tool for something else is a theme we have seen in Pater as well. "The only beautiful things, as somebody once said, are the things that do not concern us. As long as a thing is useful or necessary to us, or affects us in any way, either for pain or pleasure, or appeals strongly to our sympathies, or is a vital part of the environment in which we live, it is outside the proper sphere of art" (*Intentions*, 82). For Wilde, art is like play; it has no other end except an experience of pleasure. As soon as art becomes a tool, instrument, means to something else, it becomes something other than art.

We must observe here that, like Pater and Ruskin, Wilde does not think that ethics are nonexistent, merely that they are boring. After reading the dialogues of Vivian and Ernest one senses that Wilde himself was often bored with discussions of life, of nature, and of truth (metaphysics). Yet aesthetics do not replace or nullify ethics. Aesthetics are simply in a higher more interesting realm than ethics. In Wilde's thought, the goal

30. See Luke 10:38–42.

31. Note the difference between Wilde's view of mystics and Pater's. Pater emphasizes that they did not value their subjective experiences highly enough (in other words, they were too otherworldly), whereas Wilde emphasizes their ambivalence to ethical demands.

of every critic's life must be that exquisite experience that, along with all the other experiences gained throughout life, constitutes a new kind of mood. This mood is a synonym for religious feeling. The moralizing and teaching can be done by others, but the critic has a hieratic function that is higher than other occupations. He or she is an intercessor between the beautiful and the crowd. As a critic of the critics themselves, Wilde saw himself as such a priestly intercessor.

Beauty & Truth in *Intentions*

Where Pater repeats the noun "charm" throughout his essays, Wilde repeats the adjective "exquisite" again and again, yet both have the same pleasurable sensation with its effects in mind. Wilde holds that this experience of delightful charm or exquisite beauty is the highest aim and goal of life. For Wilde, however, the term *experience* is neither as powerful nor as accurate as the term *contemplation* in describing what the critic must strive for in her or his encounter with beauty. Through Vivian and Gilbert, Wilde declares that the contemplation of beauty is the highest aim and goal of life. It is by definition unpractical since it deals with objects that are desirable for their beauty, not for their usefulness. Similarly, this contemplation is antinomian since it deals with a spiritual sphere higher than ethics. Such contemplation is the highest occupation a person can have (*Intentions*, 175).

In his first essay of *Intentions* Wilde draws an interesting parallel to Plato: "Just as those who do not love Plato more than Truth cannot pass beyond the threshold of the Academe [*sic*], so those who do not love Beauty more than Truth never know the inmost shrine of Art" (*Intentions*, 101). In this surprising interpretation, Wilde asserts that Plato is a liar, that is, an artist, and he is more worthy of love than the truth itself. As a philosopher-artist Plato weaves beautiful myths that have enraptured people for centuries. For Wilde, Plato's words are better than truth because they are more beautiful, and although Plato would certainly disagree (probably desiring above all else to not be a liar, a sophist, a huckster), Wilde declares that Plato is a liar and should be valued for his artistic excellence. His philosophical ideas should be appreciated for their sheer beauty; all matters of actual metaphysical import may be set completely aside. The philosopher and novelist Iris Murdoch has highlighted

Plato's great artistry, which might elucidate Wilde's opinion of his artistry.[32] She writes,

> The most obvious paradox in the problem under consideration is that Plato is a great artist and produced some of the most memorable images in European philosophy: the Cave, the charioteer, the cunning homeless Eros, the Demiurge cutting the *Anima Mundi* into strips and stretching it out crosswise. He kept emphasizing the imageless remoteness of the Good, yet kept returning in his exposition to the most elaborate uses of art. . . . Art cheats the religious vocation at the last moment and is inimical to philosophical categories.[33]

Wilde is interested in art and criticism; even in relation to the great thinkers of civilization he has little regard for dogmatic "truths," whether religious or metaphysical. He is concerned with beauty, not facts: "And when that day dawns, or sunset reddens how joyous we shall all be! Facts will be regarded as discreditable, Truth will be found mourning over her fetters, and Romance, with her temper of wonder, will return to the land" (*Intentions*, 101). Romance, beauty, rapturous love—seeking after such things is the highest pursuit, and to enjoy these properly, one engages in what Wilde terms *contemplation*. These experiences of the soul then are worth far more than mere scientific facts, religious dogmas, or moral platitudes. By enjoying beauty, or lies, a person has the chance of embarking upon a life of contemplation, a life that is both meaningful and worthwhile, though utterly useless in the eyes of the world.

In "The Critic as Artist" Wilde expresses similar opinions about beauty through Gilbert as he does through Vivian. Gilbert confesses, "The longer I study, Ernest, the more clearly I see that the beauty of the visible arts is, as the beauty of music, impressive primarily, and that it may be marred, and indeed often is so, by any excess of intellectual intention on the part of the artist" (*Intentions*, 157–58). Gilbert then continues to comment upon beauty: "Beauty has as many meanings as man has

32. The nature of Plato's dramatic dialogues is a hotly debated issue in scholarship. How are his dialogues supposed to function? Is the drama simply a convenient vehicle to deliver philosophical ideas? Or is the dramaturgical structure of each dialogue crucial to its purpose? D. C. Schindler has helpfully highlighted the issues facing Plato scholars stretching back to his earliest interpreters. See Schindler, *Plato's Critique of Impure Reason*, 29–34. My point is that Wilde would dismiss all these arguments and embrace the sheer genius of the dialogues themselves as great works of art and Plato as the consummate stylist, that is, liar.

33. Murdoch, *The Fire & The Sun*, 87.

moods. Beauty is the symbol of symbols. Beauty reveals everything, because it expresses nothing. When it shows us itself, it shows us the whole fiery-coloured world" (*Intentions*, 158).

Wilde makes a significant departure from Ruskin on this point. Ruskin would argue that the greatest artist, Turner, was so great because of his massive intellect combined with his pure heart. Turner had the intellectual and moral lenses that truly received God's messages in his Book of Nature. Though Wilde follows Ruskin with the same passionate search, even obsession for beautiful things, he will have none of this moral or intellectual business. An artist does not uncover truth; an artist simply paints beautiful lies. Through his characters Wilde claims to be interested in one thing alone: the blissful experience of beauty. Yet, as I will continue to show, his search after beauty was also a response to the religious and aesthetic situation of the century. When Wilde reacts so strongly against ethics, truth, and knowledge in his interpretation of art, he is also reacting strongly against the critical spirit of the century that would prevent individuals such as him from engaging in the passionate experience of religion as, perhaps, the greatest manifestation of beauty. The next section will cover this in more detail.

Beauty & God in *Intentions*

Before continuing with an interpretation of Wilde's view of God and the Christian religion in *Intentions*, it would be worthwhile to record a few important biographical details of Wilde's religious life. Wilde's lifelong interest in theology, his yearning for some type of personal, religious fulfillment, and his deathbed reception into the Roman Catholic Church are well known and controversial matters. A major biographer notes that during Wilde's student days at Oxford, "Roman Catholicism threads its way through all Wilde's activities."[34] Indeed, this fascination with the Catholic Church did not abate, but rather culminated in dramatic events toward the end of Wilde's life. Richard Ellmann notes that on the day of his release from jail on May 19, 1897, Wilde "wrote a letter to the Jesuits at Farm Street, asking for a six-month retreat," and then when he received an answer from them, which was a refusal due to insufficient time, he

34. Ellmann, *Oscar Wilde*, 63. Also note that Wilde's early poems were mostly religious, he was a close reader of Thomas à Kempis, and he also considered Cardinal Manning to be his favorite preacher (see Ellmann, *Oscar Wilde*, 63–64).

"broke down and sobbed bitterly."[35] A few years later, while he lay upon his deathbed, a priest administered conditional baptism, absolution, and anointing.[36]

Two further points must be made here. The first is that Wilde was extremely well-read in popular and academic Christian works; he was therefore aware of century's debates surrounding the historicity of Christ's life, the authenticity of the Bible, and the origin of life on earth. He is fully conversant with much of the debate surrounding issues and overall accepts the critics' conclusions (*Intentions*, 205). The second point is that Wilde was mostly bored by all these theological squabbles raging amongst the German and British professors. What actually interests him I will lay out in this section. Since Wilde is drawn to art as a great lie, if religion is a great lie, he will gladly embrace it. In everything Wilde will freely draw from the rich prayer language of the church, including whenever appropriate, biblical quotations and mystical terminology.

In a kind of mystical passage Wilde's character Gilbert draws a comparison, like Pater, between the "art for art's sake" ideal and the scholastic theologian Abelard, "We have whispered the secret of our love beneath the cowl of Abelard, and in the stained raiment of Villon have put our shame into song. . . . Do you think that it is the imagination that enables us to live these countless lives? Yes: it is the imagination; and the imagination is the result of heredity. It is simply concentrated race-experience" (*Intentions*, 178). The imagination allows humanity to transcend time by experiencing beauty through the lives of countless critics whose experiences can be felt again through the exercise of the imagination. There is no necessity to connect the imagination to God as in Ruskin and Coleridge before him. The point is the power of the imagination itself, not its origins or theological connections. For Wilde, the nineteenth century has debunked many of these ideas regarding the imagination; critics have now reached a watershed moment where they can be released from what had previously fettered them. Wilde writes,

> The nineteenth century is a turning point in history simply on account of the work of two men, Darwin and Renan, the one the critic of the Book of Nature, the other the critic of the books of God. Not to recognize this is to miss the meaning of one of the most important eras in the progress of the world. Creation is

35. Ellmann, *Oscar Wilde*, 495.

36. Ellmann, *Oscar Wilde*, 549.

always behind the age. It is Criticism that leads us. The Critical
Spirit and the World-Spirit are one.[37]

Wilde assert this, and yet he does not really care for the theories of evolution or modern higher criticism as such. Rather, the critical urge itself, the progress of humanity itself; these are what matter most. Progress allows for the creation and critique of more and more sensations of pleasure. The critic's life then is able to transcend time, always moving humanity forward to greater saturations of exquisite beauty.

In "The Decay of Lying" Wilde makes an intriguing connection between the artist and the liar, delighting in the paradox that true art must tell lies, whereas false art can only tell truths. He writes, "For the aim of the liar is simply to charm, to delight, to give pleasure. . . . Nor will [the liar] be welcomed by society alone. Art, breaking from the prison-house of realism, will run to greet him, and will kiss his false, beautiful lips, knowing that he alone is in possession of the great secret of all her manifestations, the secret that Truth is entirely and absolutely a matter of style . . ." (*Intentions*, 88–89). When art seeks to communicate something other than its own beautiful surface, it fails; "the object of Art is not simple truth but complex beauty" (*Intentions*, 85). The artist should be unconcerned about objective religious matters; in short, he or she must be a liar, a constructor of exquisite textures and delightful colors, a manipulator of sensations and an inventor of the "mysterious loveliness" of an "incomparable and unique effect" (*Intentions*, 95).

It is in this argument for the close correspondence between lying and art that makes Wilde's comments on the established church so thought-provoking. Toward the end of the essay Wilde hammers those broad-minded, critical theologians of the century. Such theologians are the supreme doubters, according to Wilde, because they attempt to make the outrageous claims of Christianity more palatable and less objectionable to the modern sensibility. He criticizes their higher criticism and makes his character say in a flash of brilliance, "Man can believe the impossible, but man can never believe the improbable" (*Intentions*, 100). In this aphorism Wilde has given a *fin-de-siècle* version of Tertullian's famous "absurdist" credo,[38] and in the process he has discovered an

<hr>

37. Wilde, *Intentions*, 205.

38. The history of the interpretation of this credo, written in Tertullian's *De Carne Christi*, is far too complex to treat thoroughly here. Suffice it to say, some Christian authorities have dismissed Tertullian's phrase for its irrationality while others have embraced it for its challenging paradox. The famous words that Tertullian writes are

immensely important theological truth.[39] It is that religion, in order to be religion and not something else, must stand totally on its own, with all its paradoxes and contradictions. The impossible is beautiful; the improbable never is.

Wilde has, in a sense, put his finger on the pulse of religious skepticism in the late nineteenth century; he has shown that true religion is an art. When it is claiming to teach society something, standing above the populace as a lecturer and judge, it is boring. When it bravely embodies beauty in itself and thus lives out an impossible ideal, then it, too, is exquisite. Wilde decides that there is a great similarity between religious expression and artistic expression. He thinks religion should act like art, and when it does tell a lie, it must fearlessly tell a beautiful and complex one. For in theorizing and arguing points of dogma, religion is sounding *improbable* and thus opening itself to all kinds of critique. The power and force of religion lies in this beautiful quality of its impossibility.

Yet Wilde finds himself in a conundrum of how to accept the beautiful lie that Christianity is. Chesterton describes this key aspect of Wilde in a 1908 essay included in the previously mentioned collection, *A Handful of Authors*: "But while he had a strain of humbug in him . . . he had, in his own strange way, a much deeper and more spiritual nature than they. . . . He desired all beautiful things, even God."[40] This is the paradox in "The Decay of Lying" that Wilde leaves intriguingly unresolved. In the late nineteenth century, Wilde could see Christianity adapting itself to modern sensibilities, modifying its claims as a response to scientific and geological discoveries. But if the Christian church accommodates itself to the modern world in order to sound less fantastic and more reasonable, then it instantly becomes more boring for Oscar Wilde. It is precisely in these projects of accommodation that religion joins all the other drab clubs and systems that try to sound convincing and win arguments. Wilde would prefer the Christian religion simply to "be": to express itself without dealing in society's arguments of rational truth. When the church deals in truths it is stooping to "unimaginative realism" when Wilde would have it engage in "imaginative reality" (*Intentions*, 81). Again, "Man can believe the impossible, but man can never believe

---

these (as translated by Osborn): "The son of God has died: this is believable because it is silly; buried he has risen again: this is certain because it is impossible." See Osborn, *Tertullian*, 48.

39. See Chesterton, *A Handful of Authors*, 146.

40. See above for my first reference to this interesting work.

the improbable" (*Intentions*, 100). Wilde would only have this type of belief—glorious and beautiful in its sheer impossibility.

In "The Critic as Artist" Wilde again explores theology, making comparisons between artistic expression and traditional Christianity and using the language of the church in his discussion of art. His character Ernest has the ultimate aim of living a life of critical contemplation. Contemplation opens up "the subjective sphere where the soul is at work" (*Intentions*, 176). It is therefore to be contrasted with the life of action, of creation. This has echoes of the classic Gospel story of Martha the busybody and Mary the contemplative. Martha works while her sister contemplates, loves, and adores Jesus Christ.[41]

Wilde's essay contains a further echo of the New Testament in his description of this contemplative life: "And so it is not our own life that we live, but the lives of the dead, and the soul that dwells within us is no single spiritual entity" (*Intentions*, 176).[42] Wilde goes on to say that this contemplative life "has for its aim not *doing* but *being*, and not being merely, but *becoming* . . ." (*Intentions*, 178, italics original).[43] The life of the critic is far deeper than doing busy work. It is, rather, an experience of becoming something that transcends boundaries and worlds. It is also a process that takes the past and the future into itself, transcending all times in a kind of spiritual experience.[44] For Wilde, to be a critic is to be a part of a process larger than conventional religion, with the puritanism and narrowness he perceives in it. Wilde's process is actually one that begins with contemplation and culminates in a deep transformation. He is consciously mimicking biblical language and making biblical allusions, perhaps only to provoke his opponents, and yet, perhaps he is also drawing a parallel between the nature of religion in its most beautiful manifestations and art in its most beautiful manifestations. Contemplation, whether it is of a Catholic relic or secular painting, must involve a person's entire existence. When such existential contemplation deals with

41. See Luke 10:40.

42. Whether this is intentional or not, Wilde uses Pauline language, as found in Galatians 2:20, "It is no longer I who live, but Christ who lives in me."

43. Here Wilde writes with an almost Pauline emphasis on sanctification and holy transformation; see 2 Corinthians 3:18.

44. Could Wilde have in mind the Christian idea of a "cloud of witnesses"—all those believers across time, which connect with faithful believers in the present? The New Testament reference is from Hebrews 12:1a: "Therefore, since we are surrounded by so great a cloud of witnesses, let us also lay aside every weight. . . ."

anything other than the object in its sheer beauty, when it deals in truth claims and arguments, logic and morality, rather than pure aesthesis, then the contemplation comes to an end and the critic has failed. Wilde's language on aesthetic contemplation sounds similar to the Christian practice of contemplative prayer, focused on God in the purity of a pure, loving gaze.[45]

At the end of "The Critic as Artist," Wilde's character Gilbert has something almost akin to a religious vision. He says passionately to Ernest,

> Aesthetics, like sexual selection, make life lovely and wonderful, fill it with new forms, and give it progress, and variety and change. And when we reach the true culture that is our aim, we attain that perfection of which the saints have dreamed, the perfection of those to whom sin is impossible, not because they make the renunciations of the ascetic, but because they can do everything they wish without hurt to the soul, and can wish for nothing that can do the soul harm, the soul being an entity so divine that it is able to transform into elements of a richer experience, or a finer susceptibility, or a newer mode of thought, acts or passions that with the common would be commonplace, or with the uneducated ignoble, or with the shameful vile. Is this dangerous? Yes; it is dangerous—all ideas, as I told you, are so.[46]

Wilde says that the "true culture" of a passionate aesthetic is the aim of life and, if attained, will lead to a kind of worldly perfection. Wilde's vocabulary, with words such as "perfection," "saints," "ascetics," and "divine," is not used in mockery of religion, but in demonstrating that aesthetic experience underlies the deepest religious experiences. Such experiences are always aesthetic; that is, they involve vision and the "seeing" of something. Art is then deeply, truly, fundamentally religious—more religious than either that "unimaginative realism" of traditional, dogmatic, puritanical Christianity or the soft and accommodating Christianity of the modern theologians. Art is religious, because it allows women and men to contemplate transformative, rapturous beauty—even if that beauty is God or Christ in Catholicism.

---

45. Thomas Merton, the celebrated spiritual guide and Trappist monk, talks of contemplation as "the abandonment of other concerns" as well as an "attitude of awareness and receptivity." The goal of contemplation "is not to arrive at an objective and apparently 'scientific' knowledge about God." See Merton, *Contemplative Prayer*, 19, 41, 82. The similarities between Wilde and the classic, monastic practice of contemplation/adoration are intriguing.

46. Wilde, *Intentions*, 205.

The implication in of all this is that while the saints may have dreamed of such a perfect life, Wilde thinks they failed to realize that their religion was not anything *higher than* those imaginative, beautiful, and exquisite moments and experiences. Such experiences were the heart and very substance of their religion. These ideas coming from Gilbert's mouth might be considered as dangerous to the established church because they overthrow any kind of purely cultural or purely doctrinal Christianity. The membership of such a church is not adherence to rules but contemplation of perfect beauty. Wilde exemplified this in his final religious quest. For if the most meaningful experiences of life are those moments of aesthetic contemplation, then those who do not find these enriching, exquisite experiences are not fully alive and not fully believers in the *impossible*.

Where does Wilde's religion begin and his aestheticism end? About Wilde's free mixing of beauty and God throughout his career, Ellmann writes that he set forth an aestheticism that embraced religion:

> He did this not by rejecting aesthetics or ethics, but by turning sacred things inside out to make them secular, and secular things inside out to make them sacred. He showed souls becoming carnal and lusts becoming spiritual. He showed the aesthetic world not isolated from experience, but infused into it. This was the new Hellenism of which he liked to speak.[47]

For both Pater and Wilde, the lure of Hellenism is pervasive. Hellenism for them meant a religion of the surface, a celebration of the flesh. There is no question for them that while Ruskin did very valuable work, his oppressive doctrine of theoria, born from his interest in natural theology, must be discarded in the face of a radically new age. But in the "art for art's sake" camp, the beauties of religion, whether Greek or Christian, and the glories of Catholicism, whether built, painted, or sung, are just too exquisite to be utterly rejected.

Wilde's Yearning for God

In our consideration of *Intentions*, we have seen that Wilde has treated beauty's relation to morality, truth, and God in similar ways to Pater. He has separated morality and religion from aesthetics, but then he nearly puts them back together again in a religious-aesthetic synthesis—his

47. Ellman, *Oscar Wilde*, 340–41.

religion of the delicate surface, his Hellenism. In this acceptance of the paradox of the impossible, in this continued echo of biblical language, in this yearning for deep contemplation, and in this dissatisfaction with all attempts at softening the Christian message, Wilde engages in what seems like a deeply religious yearning for beauty. Yet this is a radically new understanding of all religious experience. It is therefore also a harsh and critical reevaluation the type of Christianity that seemed to be retreating from critics such as Strauss and Renan in nineteenth-century England. Paul Guyer's estimation of Wilde's *Intentions* is worth quoting at length:

> Far from being an aesthete who believed in the independence of art and aesthetic experience from every other human concern, Wilde in fact conceived art as a medium for the fullest exercise of human imagination, the communication of the broadest possible range of human emotions, and for the exploration of the deepest truths about morality rather than for the celebration of superficial social conventions. He thus did not take the slogan "art for art's sake" as the banner of a reductive or isolationist approach to aesthetic experience, but rather took it to express the power that art can have precisely when it exploits all these possibilities.[48]

Ruskin's theoria and Pater and Wilde's aesthesis thus occupy different ends of a spectrum. With Ruskin there comes a highly ordered and systematic process whereby we apprehend a Creator God through his channels in beautiful, sublime nature. Those who have "eyes to see" are the artists and observers that can faithfully receive this truth before communicating it to those who might not have the capacities to receive it without instruction. Theoria is the (morally) pure reception of God's truths disclosed in the natural realm. It is a spiritual-aesthetic perception focused upon a providential Creator who dwells in the heavens but can be known by his works. I have argued that Ruskin's conception of God at the center of beauty, as both beauty's origin and beauty's *telos*, functions as a kind of aesthetic, natural theology. Pater and Wilde seek to purify Ruskin's theology of anything but the sheer draw of beauty itself, and so they occupy the other end of this spectrum. The aesthetes shed (almost) all vestiges of established religion and raise the glory of fleshly, earthly humanity above nature. They focus upon contemplation, especially with its mystical and deeply Catholic overtones. Their "art for art's sake" aesthetic renders passionate worship to the surface, to the body, to the outward glories

48. Guyer, *A History of Modern Aesthetics*, 2:269.

of things, but it seems that this is not enough for either Pater or Wilde. There is in their writings this abiding openness to something greater, above the surfaces of things, or something deeper, binding all beautiful things together.

This leads us to turn our attention, by contrast, to the critic at the end of the "long nineteenth century" (1789–1914) who, perhaps more than any other popular writer and critic at this time, fully realized that the paths of theoria and aesthesis did not adequately answer the post-Kantian challenges of Strauss, Renan, and other critics of the century. He gave an answer neither in apologetic natural theology nor in an elevation of beauty to religion, but in his pointing to the beautiful and symbolically rich sacramental encounter in the very notion of art itself. As we will see, Chesterton's aesthetic approach to religion highlights the idea that an artist, in all of her or his unique creativity, is an image of a mysterious, artistic God.

3

Symbolism

Chesterton and the Symbolist Movement

GILBERT KEITH CHESTERTON (1874–1936) was not an influential art theorist in his day, and he is generally not regarded as either a professional philosopher or theologian. Yet, Chesterton should be of immense interest to scholars and students of aesthetics, for in his own way he brought together Victorian approaches to beauty and religion, critiqued them, and synthesized them into his own symbolist and sacramental aesthetic. In this chapter, I focus upon several works of art criticism by this brilliant journalist. Beginning with a handful of almost unknown essays published in *The Bookman* and *Daily News* from 1900–1901, I also interpret his two small books written on individual painters, *G. F. Watts* (1904) and *William Blake* (1910), which are largely neglected today. In my analysis of these texts, I show why it is legitimate to situate Chesterton broadly within the symbolist movement of the turn of the century, and I then demonstrate how Chesterton recovers a Catholic and mystical tradition in the wake of the religious and aesthetic fragmentation in the Victorian age. Chesterton affirms the divine, sacramental presence in the physical and offers a revalidation of Christian belief in mystery and magic. His basis for faith is not natural theology, as in Ruskin, or an affirmation of the religious-like experience of beauty, as in Pater and Wilde, but rather, it is an intuitive divine experience, or sacred encounter, mediated through words, symbols, and sacraments. In making my argument in this chapter, I must first uncover what the symbolist movement was and then suggest ways to broadly situate Chesterton within the movement.

The symbolist movement in poetry and the arts originates from within late Romanticism and follows the spirit of Hegelianism in some ways with its focus upon eternal Spirit penetrating into the temporal world in sweeping, creative epochs.[1] Broadly speaking, the poets and artists who identified as "symbolist" wished for the arts to recover myth, magic, religion, and ritual as the sources of human creativity and the outward manifestation of eternal ideas. First heralded in the *Symbolist Manifesto* (1886), by poet Jean Moréas, the symbolist movement originated in France among poets who rejected Zola and other realists.[2] Baudelaire, whom we encountered previously as one of the major influences on the aesthetes, was also a significant forerunner of the French symbolists. In a passage illustrative of his symbolism, he writes, "[T]he whole of the visible universe is only a storehouse of images and signs to which the imagination assigns a place and a relative value; it is a kind of nourishment that the imagination must digest and transform."[3] Baudelaire's belief is that artistic symbols—whether in poetry, the visual arts, or other avenues—serve as gateways to higher worlds and indicators of eternal truth. Baudelaire and his ideas strongly resonated with many of the English Romantics and, by extension, our four critics who read them widely.[4]

This Romantic notion of the power of symbols exerted a strong influence throughout the century. Figures like Blake, Coleridge, and Shelley were sources of inspiration and fascination for Ruskin and his successors. With the Paterian call of "art for art's sake," the beautiful symbol *itself* became an object of interest, even of worship, taking the place of the higher truths the symbol might indicate. For, as we have seen in the previous chapter, the aesthetes elevated the here-and-now material beauty of a work of art, not denying the power of symbols as such, but denying the power of such symbols to lead the mind *beyond them to truths*, whether Christian or otherwise. The call of "art for art's sake" meant that the symbol, if it is a beautiful one, might be enjoyed or even worshiped for its own sake. A new religion of beauty could be one "beyond the spiritual system" as Pater and Wilde phrased it.

1. Graham and Hough, *Strangeness and Beauty*, 2:162.

2. Chipp, *Theories of Modern Art*, 48. Also worth noting is that Chesterton excoriates Zola in a number of essays and book chapters; for example, see chapter II of *Heretics*, "On the Negative Spirit," where Chesterton compares Zola's realism to the bleak reality that the devil or hangman would signify.

3. Chipp, *Theories of Modern Art*, 49.

4. Graham and Hough, *Strangeness and Beauty*, 1:170.

With the symbolist movement comes a return in the arts to this earlier, Romantic vision of the symbol. As Coleridge was the conduit for German idealism into England in the beginning of the nineteenth century, the English writer Arthur Symons was the conduit for French symbolism into England in the late nineteenth century. Symons's seminal work *The Symbolist Movement in Literature* (1899) was especially influential. In this work, dedicated to his friend W. B. Yeats, Symons mediates the French symbolist rediscovery of mysticism, magic, and Catholicism. Symons argues that, during the loss of interest in symbolism in the last century, Paterian aestheticism simply led to the Decadent movement, which is just an "interlude" to the more important development of symbolism; it is in symbolism that "art returns to the one pathway, leading through beautiful things to the eternal beauty."[5] Here Symons is moving past both Pater and Wilde as well as the Decadent movement, which was the conclusion of the "art for art's sake" credo. For Symons returns again and again in his work to the *mystery* that underlies all forms of expression, all human creativity. "The ideal of lyric poetry, certainly, is to be this passive, flawless medium for the deeper consciousness of things, the mysterious voice of that mystery which lies about us, out of which we have come, and into which we shall all return. It is not without reason that we cannot analyse a perfect lyric."[6]

Symons argues that the world is irrationally, inexplicably mysterious, and the only force that comes close to providing a pathway through it is art. Along with the later symbolists, Symons does not believe art can be reduced to colors or poetry reduced to mere words. Rather, art and poetry are concerned with expressing the irreducible mystery of *something else*—something far higher. However, this "something else" is not simply a moral system. Symons is neither concerned with a "guide for conduct" nor a "plan for our happiness";[7] he is, rather, concerned with "that confidence in the eternal correspondences between the visible and the invisible universe," which the French symbolist poets such as Mallarmé had taught.[8] In a concluding chapter titled "Maeterlinck as Mystic" (in his first edition), Symons writes that "the whole aim of Maeterlinck[9] is

5. Symons, *The Symbolist Movement in Literature*, 7.

6. Symons, *The Symbolist Movement in Literature*, 46.

7. Symons, *The Symbolist Movement in Literature*, 89.

8. Symons, *The Symbolist Movement in Literature*, 71.

9 Maurice Maeterlinck (1862–1949) was a Belgian author who was a leading figure in the symbolist movement. See Drabble, *Oxford Companion to English Literature*, 606.

to show how mysterious all life is, 'what an astounding thing it is, merely to live.'"[10] Chesterton shares many of Symons's sensibilities, as an illustrative essay on Maeterlinck at the turn of the century reveals. Reprinted in the compilation titled *Varied Types* (1903), Chesterton considers Maeterlinck to be "a very great man," for he is a writer who has brought back a "subjective intensity" by which the human soul is revealed again as an "indestructible thing."[11] Chesterton goes on to write, "This human soul finds itself alone in a terrible world, afraid of the grass. It has brought forth poetry and religion in order to explain matters; it will bring them forth again."[12] Here the concern is for Maeterlinck's kind of rediscovery of the soul, that invisible universe. Like Symons, Chesterton appreciates the French symbolists for their desire for a return to spiritual matters of ultimate importance through literature and art. Whether it is mysticism, Catholicism, eastern religions, Theosophy, or magic, the symbolist writers and artists share a more or less common vision that the present (circa 1900) must be a time of recovering those vital, spiritual sources of life and creativity. In addition to affinities with Symons and Maeterlinck, Chesterton also has close ties with Yeats. I will explore this in more detail after offering interpretations of Chesterton's early essays of art criticism—essays that demonstrate Chesterton's many sympathies with this influential literary and artistic movement.

Chesterton's Early Art Criticism

A fairly large selection of very early essays (i.e., pieces written before *Heretics* was published in 1905) demonstrate Chesterton's link to symbolism. For my purposes, I will focus on essays that deal with works of art or individual painters, specifically from early paid work for *The Bookman* and then from the *Daily News*.

Chesterton found some of his earliest paid journalistic work writing reviews of art books for *The Bookman*, which was a magazine of book reviews, self-described as "A monthly Journal for Bookreaders, Bookbuyers, and Booksellers [*sic*]."[13] Most of these reviews were short pieces of only a few paragraphs regarding whichever new biography or

10. Symons, *The Symbolist Movement in Literature*, 80.
11. Chesterton, *Varied Types*, 214.
12. Chesterton, *Varied Types*, 214.
13. Chesterton and Hodder Williams, *Thomas Carlyle*, inside leaf.

illustrated work Chesterton was handed to read and review. These brief review pieces have such titles as "Velasquez and Poussin," "The Renaissance and Modern Art," and "Correggio." These pieces from 1899 and early 1900 contained a few witty observations, but were, by their nature, too short to afford the young journalist an opportunity to develop his critical and aesthetic theories. Chesterton had this chance a number of book reviews later, when he wrote several longer and more developed essays for *The Bookman*. From June 1900 to December 1901 Chesterton produced no less than five substantial essays on contemporary artists and their paintings: the three-part "Literary Pictures of the Year" (coauthored with a friend, J. E. Hodder Williams), "Famous Novelists in the National Portrait Gallery," and "The Literary Portraits of G. F. Watts, R.A."[14] These essays are hardly ever mentioned in biographies or studies on Chesterton, probably because of their early date and uncollected status.[15] Yet they reveal a great deal about the development of Chesterton's early critical and aesthetic views, especially in relation to the ideas put forward by the three other writers in this study.

Chesterton, who was twenty-six years old in 1900, shows an early interest in three problems of aesthetics: the relationship between painting and literature (the image and the word), the morality or immorality of art, and, most importantly, the union of the physical with the spiritual in art. In the eyes of his contemporaries, artist-critics such as James McNeill Whistler[16] and George Moore,[17] such an effort by a young journalist to marry the two arts and then to see in them some kind of correspondence

14. Chesterton articulates the core themes, which he would expand three years later into his book titled *G. F. Watts* (1904). The arguments Chesterton makes in this essay reveal a great deal about the development of his early critical and aesthetic views, especially in relation to the ideas put forward by the three other writers in this study.

15. The more recent biographers, such as Ker and Oddie, mention them only in relation to Chesterton's biographical details, specifically the path Chesterton took during his career as journalist from one publication to another. They do not appear in recently published collections of Chesterton's essays or reviews. The two most significant recent collections and republications of Chesterton's essays are: Stapleton, *G. K. Chesterton at the Daily News*, and Chesterton, *The Illustrated London News* (G. K. Chesterton Collected Works). Many of Chesterton's other essays appear in separately published collections such as *Varied Types*, etc., while others still remain uncollected.

16. For more on Whistler, see my Introduction.

17. George Augustus Moore (1852–1933) was an Anglo-Irish novelist who had studied painting in Paris. His writing was inspirited by Emile Zola and other nineteenth-century French realists. See Drabble, "Moore," in *The Oxford Companion to English Literature*, 665.

to metaphysics would have seemed hopelessly out-of-date. Yet Chesterton, like Yeats his close friend,[18] entered the century with strong reactions to the aesthetes and the decadents. In these early essays we thus see a young critic trying to reconnect image to word, morality to art, and humanity to God. It is the last combination, humanity to God, where Chesterton forms a synthesis of Ruskin's theological views with the aesthetes' material views. I will argue that this synthesis is held together by Chesterton's Christian faith and his strong notion of sacramentality—the hiddenness or interpenetration of spirit and flesh, word with material.

Truly, it is in these early, short pieces, often around a page in length, that Chesterton begins developing some of his earliest critical and aesthetic ideas that would find their way into nearly all of his later works of criticism, including books on individual poets and novelists,[19] as well as many hundreds of essays. These early critical essays give Chesterton his first opportunity to develop his ideas relating Ruskin, Pater, and Wilde. Because of the concentration of aesthetic arguments, the early date, and the inattention given to them by scholars, I am choosing to closely examine them rather than any of Chesterton's more famous works, which also tend to give a great many aesthetic reflections.

Interestingly, it is in these early essays that Chesterton develops what is perhaps one of his more important contributions to twentieth-century aesthetics, a contribution that has been virtually overlooked by scholars of the symbolist movement and of Chesterton. This is the idea of the complex, push-and-pull relationship of word and image. To put it simply, in Chesterton's mind, stories and pictures do not inhabit separate realms that never mingle; instead, word and image continually interact and impregnate one another. In a sense, one cannot comprehend any idea apart from this interplay of both words and pictures. Art historians and philosophers of aesthetics after Chesterton have actually seen this to be the case as well, and they echo much of what Chesterton noticed in 1900. For example, Mieke Bal, in her seminal book *Reading Rembrandt: Beyond the Word–Image Opposition*, could be described as engaging in a Chestertonian exploration when she writes, "For, in an important sense, an image is not a text; but while irreducibly different, the visual and the verbal domains interpenetrate, influence, and inform each other."[20] She

18. More on this below.

19. See Chesterton, *Robert Browning*.

20. Bal, *Reading Rembrandt*, 19.

goes on to point out that images can never merely illustrate something because they become, in themselves, a new text: "So the image does not replace a text; it *is* one."[21] Bal and Chesterton share a very similar outlook. Chesterton's purpose in relating the two arts of literature and painting over and over again is to demonstrate the power that images and words have in a creative unity, while working together in tandem.

The first three essays of 1900, coauthored with J. E. Hodder Williams, and are titled "Literary Pictures of the Year."[22] In the pieces, the writers examine recent pictures from the Royal Academy that deal with literary subjects, critiquing their relation to the literary characters or qualities they interact with. Even though, for the most part, the artists they mention, including Amelia Bauerle, Edwin Austin Abbey, Arthur Rackham, Cyrus Cuneo, John da Costa, Mabel Ashby, and Nell Tenison, are not exactly household names today, the article is intriguing because of its adaptation and transformation of the (increasingly) established "art for art's sake" aesthetic.

Critiquing many recent paintings that take their subject matter from works of literature, Chesterton and Hodder Williams also critique the philosophy of Ruskin, Pater, and Wilde at every step of the way. The first part of this essay has the subtitle "I—Shakespeare, Tennyson, Dickens," revealing three giants whom Chesterton would draw much of his inspiration from for the rest of his career. The authors waste no time in getting straight to the point: "In the year's art taken as a whole, there are signs of a healthy reaction in the relation between painting and literature; and it is a matter upon which saner ideas are really needed."[23] With these words the authors situate their argument within the current aesthetic context. This will be an article that critiques aesthetic viewpoints as well as particular works of art that deal with scenes, characters, and quotations from the three authors mentioned in the title. The reason that these two must write such an article in the first place is because they see in their time "the tyranny of a dogma equally fantastic and illogical—the notion that the two arts may not even be allied, as poetry and music are in a song."[24] Chesterton and his friend do not seek to prove the superiority of one art form over another, as virtually all previous aestheticians from

21. Bal, *Reading Rembrandt*, 34–35.

22. Chesterton and Hodder Williams, "Literary Pictures of the Year," 79–84.

23. Chesterton and Hodder Williams, "Literary Pictures of the Year," 79.

24. Chesterton and Hodder Williams, "Literary Pictures of the Year," 79.

Schelling to Wilde had done. Rather, Chesterton and Hodder Williams take a very nuanced approach to painting and literature. As we have seen, Walter Pater believed poetry, music, and painting each had its own "peculiar and untranslatable charm," that is to say, these creative acts are not three modes that are equally capable of expressing the same truth; they do not mingle and cannot be weighed against each other in terms of the moral and metaphysical truths they express.[25] Whistler takes the "art for art's sake" doctrine a step farther when he argues in his influential "10 O'Clock Lecture" that a painting must never be interpreted as if it were a story or poem, for this makes it a means to an end; art absolutely cannot be translated from canvas to paper.[26] Now, this sense that art has a kind of poetic power is found in the world of those influenced by German idealists: Coleridge, Shelley, Wordsworth, Ruskin, and Emerson. It follows the general idealist belief in the ability of art to act as the *organon* of philosophy, disclosing truths of the Spirit as poetry is also able to accomplish. Whistler and the decadents are therefore challenging these established, Romantic opinions. So in this article we see Chesterton and Hodder Williams challenging the decadent view, restoring to art its higher, symbolic powers. This propensity to symbolism and to the aims of the movement is revealed when they discuss Shakespeare:

> All other poets give a general sense of decorative unity—he alone is in love with contrasts, the contrasts of figure landscape and costume which make practical pictures. Touchstone and the Shepherd, Bottom and the Fairies, Lear and the Fool, Hamlet and the Gravediggers, are all scenes in which the moral irony is expressed in definite diversities of colour and form. And in this he is qualified to unite the arts. He is a symbolist: he represents the mysterious mental connection between shapes and ideas, which must finally defeat any purely technical view of painting. A man can no more see certain clouds at evening without growing thoughtful than he can see a Bengal tiger without jumping. Both feelings are equally primal, fundamental, anthropological.[27]

Shakespeare was a symbolist, and there is a "mysterious mental connection between shapes and ideas"; with this line the authors affirm an

25. See Pater, *The Renaissance*, 130.

26. See Whistler, "10 O'Clock Lecture," included in Warner and Hough, *Strangeness and Beauty*, 2:82.

27. Chesterton and Hodder Williams, "Literary Pictures of the Year," 80.

aesthetic from earlier in the century that clashes with the "art for art's sake" movement, and they implicitly suggest that a symbolist view of the arts may save the connections between the arts that is threatening to be destroyed completely.

Now onto the second installment of this three-part essay: "Literary Pictures of the Year: II—The Three Classes of Literary Art."[28] A key line in Chesterton's symbolism comes in the praise of a painting for William Morris's romance tale, "Rapunzel," by Isobel Lilian Gloag, a frequent painter of mermaids and fairies. In this painting, which so effectively "represents the medieval revival," Chesterton somewhat humorously declares, "There is more of Pre-Raphaelite ethics in the mere looking down from a tower upon the woods and towns of earth than in ten chapters of John Ruskin."[29] Rapunzel looking down, waiting for her love, is neither simply a good old tale that people enjoy nor a pretense for a metaphysical message; it is, rather, a *symbol*. To Chesterton (and Hodder Williams), the overall power of the symbol's meaning is left to the reader to feel, but it is certain that it will be deeper than ten chapters of moralistic teaching such as the kind the writers find in Ruskin.

This second installment of the essay contains the writers' main thesis, that the judgment of pictures must not only come from an aesthetic point of view, but also from a literary and ethical one. After declaring "we do not think, strictly speaking, there is any such thing as a *work* of art" (italics mine), since art enters into every human activity whatsoever, Chesterton and Hodder Williams then divide all literary art into three broad groups: "those pictures in which the literary idea is the inspiration, those in which it is a legitimate pretext, and those in which it is, unless we are much mistaken, a mere afterthought."[30] From this they go on to discuss the artist of literary pictures who is second only to G. F. Watts: Briton Rivière, specifically his work on St. George. They write, "Mr Rivière's picture, on the other hand, seems to us an excellent example of the first class of poetical pictures, the class in which the poetical idea is really the inspiring and controlling force. The colours and lines of the picture are not, so to speak, blind interpreters, they are plenipotentiary

28. See Chesterton and Hodder Williams, "Literary Pictures of the Year, II—The Three Classes of Literary Art," 112–16.

29. Chesterton and Hodder Williams, "Literary Pictures of the Year, II—The Three Classes of Literary Art," 115.

30. Chesterton and Hodder Williams, "Literary Pictures of the Year, II—The Three Classes of Literary Art," 112.

ministers of the idea; themselves full of its spirit."[31] About this painting they go on to say,

> If the picture were seen in the distance, the mere scheme of colour, the red of the flowers as hot as fire, the blue of the sea, that blue which is hotter than any red, would signal to the spectator who had not yet seen the figures of the Princess bending over her fainting or dying deliverer, the presence of that moral intoxication to which death and destruction seem as beautiful as sea and flowers.[32]

The notion of a "blue hotter than red" would be nonsense to Ruskin, while the very idea of a "literary picture" would be dismissed as a concept by the aesthetes.

In the final part of this essay, "Literary Pictures of the Year II—The Three Classes of Literary Art—(continued),"[33] Chesterton and Hodder Williams continue their exploration of the various ways that artists draw from literature and poetry. In their previous essay from June, they had discussed works based on particular scenes and literary quotations; now they deal with pictures that use titles drawn from literary works, but do not actually offer meaningful interpretations of those works. This is the lowest kind of literary art with titles "[that] are thrown off almost as a kind of humorous apology," that function more like a "bow of introduction" before the work they reference.[34] One such picture, by Sidney Meteyard, depicts Omar Khayyam in a decidedly modern fashion; taking the line "Wine is a melted ruby; the cup is the mine" as his starting place, the artist has painted an "unfathomably dismal" Omar who appears to be drinking cod-liver oil rather than wine; Chesterton wastes no opportunity to critique the aesthetes: "We are well aware that Omar was an unhappy man, as every man always was and always will be who tries to manufacture happiness out of pleasure—sunbeams out of cucumbers."[35]

31. Chesterton and Hodder Williams, "Literary Pictures of the Year, II—The Three Classes of Literary Art," 113.

32. Chesterton and Hodder Williams, "Literary Pictures of the Year, II—The Three Classes of Literary Art," 113.

33. Chesterton and Hodder Williams, "Literary Pictures of the Year: II—The Three Classes of Literary Art—(Continued)," 141–42.

34. Chesterton and Hodder Williams, "Literary Pictures of the Year: II—The Three Classes of Literary Art—(Continued)," 141.

35. Chesterton and Hodder Williams, "Literary Pictures of the Year: II—The Three Classes of Literary Art—(Continued)," 141. Also see Chesterton, *Heretics*, 102–9. This is the "Omar and the Sacred Vine" chapter.

For Chesterton (and Hodder Williams), pleasure cannot be a source of happiness nor can it provide the answer to the riddle of life. The aesthetes are therefore wrong when they say that life is worth living only because of the experience of pleasurable, exquisite moments.

The fourth early essay that is important for developing a picture of Chesterton as an art critic is from December 1900, "The Literary Portraits of G. F. Watts, R.A."[36] This essay is the core of the book that Chesterton will write in 1904 on the misunderstood, deeply allegorical painter. In the essay Chesterton again takes up the subject of portraiture, something that would remain a fascination to him throughout his life. According to Chesterton, the "school of l'art pour l'art" takes an issue with Watts's allegorical paintings but can praise his portraits, doubtlessly because this aesthetic school would appreciate the surface of the portrait, devoid of any other subject except the face and body presented.[37] By this he implies that the aesthetic school would take issue with Watts's openly allegorical paintings, in which various human urges, such as hope or greed, are represented by animals, expressions, various objects, and so forth. Chesterton decides not just to interpret Watts's obvious allegories, but to interpret all of his portraits—even those paintings that the aesthetes supposedly can tolerate—in a decidedly allegorical, symbolist way. Chesterton argues that Watts's portraits and, indeed, all artists' portraits, *cannot but* be spiritual and allegorical. Hidden truths are *always* there beneath the artistic elements of a portrait. Chesterton explains why this is:

> All the portraits are allegories for the simple reason that all men are allegories, puzzles, earthly stories with heavenly meanings: the difference between them is mainly in degree of lucidity, in the fact that while some are as stately as a pageant of Spenser, as plain and passionate as a dialogue of Bunyan, or as quaint and philosophical as a fable of Æsop, some others of our acquaintances are somewhat murky designs by William Blake, from which the heavenly meaning is exceedingly difficult to extract. The profoundly original and enduring quality of Mr. Watts' portraits lies in this, that he always paints the portrait of a modern man, who wears a silk hat and pays taxes, as if he were painting a purely elemental and cosmic subject.[38]

36. Chesterton, "The Literary Portraits of G. F. Watts, R.A.," 80–83.
37. Chesterton, "The Literary Portraits of G. F. Watts, R.A.," 80.
38. Chesterton, "The Literary Portraits of G. F. Watts, R.A.," 80.

Chesterton's critical terminology is far from being technical in these early essays—he uses the words "symbol," "allegory," "puzzle," and "riddle" nearly synonymously; by any of these words he means basically the same thing. So portraits, which are essentially symbolical, have the power of uncovering or revealing the spiritual essence of the sitter. As allegories, physical appearances outline spiritual natures. Watts's portraiture is thus able to penetrate deeply into human essence, and all portraits in general have a fantastic symbolic power as they bring out the metaphysical truth of humanity that has existed since before artists picked up their paintbrushes. In a humorous passage, which also contains a kind of mystical turn, Chesterton writes, "As we gaze at this gallery of almost heroic figures, the strange fancy grows on us that the portraits were invented before the people: that they are archetypes, designs from the terrible sketch-book of Nature. Some of the actual people have certainly lost by reproduction."[39]

For the way that Chesterton praises Watts, it may then come as no surprise that Chesterton would be moved to write an entire book on the artist a few years later. Chesterton never loses sight of the metaphysical ideas behind every painting; he sees everything as symbolic. Praising Watts for having this same sort of inclination, he writes, "But Watts, alone among artists, has never, to our knowledge, painted a picture, however old the subject, without adding to it a definite idea, strong enough to be a motive for throwing away a cigar, or getting out of an armchair."[40] Watts's artworks are certainly not vehicles that deliver bare didactic lessons, but Chesterton observes that they always do communicate some kind of "a definite idea." Throwing away a cigar is an example of a kind of visceral, natural, human reaction caused by the experience of a powerful idea, an

39. Chesterton, "The Literary Portraits of G. F. Watts, R.A.," 80.

40. Chesterton, "The Literary Portraits of G. F. Watts, R.A.," 82. This image of a man being so moved that he does something with his cigar is one that Chesterton uses elsewhere. In his essay "Secret of a Train" he relates the following story; once as he was riding a train he was enjoying a cigar. When the stoker told him that the train was carrying a corpse, Chesterton immediately extinguished his cigar. Reflecting on this, he writes, "Something that is as old as man and has to do with all mourning and ceremonial told me to do it. There was something unnecessarily horrible, it seemed to me, in the idea of there being only two men in that train, one of them dead and the other smoking a cigar. And as the red and gold of the butt end of it faded like a funeral torch trampled out at some symbolic moment of a procession, I realised how immortal ritual is. I realised (what is the origin and essence of all ritual) that in the presence of those sacred riddles about which we can say nothing it is often more decent merely to do something." See Chesterton, *Tremendous Trifles*, 23.

upsetting or surprising truth. These definite ideas lie behind every act of creation.

The fifth and final essay I wish to examine from *The Bookman* is titled "Famous Novelists in the National Portrait Gallery" from December 1901.[41] In it, Chesterton continues to develop his ideas on the relation between word and image as well as the power of allegory, or symbolism, in literature and portrait painting. In this essay Chesterton is concerned with the close connection, or rather inter-relationship, between the arts of painting (specifically that of portraiture) with literature. We hear some by-now familiar ideas when he writes,

> We speak of allegorical in art, but all art, without any exception, is allegorical. The only distinction that exists is between two kinds of allegorical art, the lower allegorical art in which certain figures or images represent certain qualities already named and classified, in which faith is called a knight and temptation a dragon, and the higher allegorical art in which certain images express dark beauties that have never been investigated and wild truths that have never been tamed.[42]

What Chesterton calls "the higher allegorical art" is set apart from a more simplistic symbolism—where a character, concept, or theme gives flesh in some sense to a theme or idea. The higher allegory is something much more akin to a deeper, Coleridgean notion of symbolism, where certain images bring forth something deeper, more primordial and mysterious than themselves: those "dark beauties" and "wild truths" that are, perhaps, too dark and too wild to even be named. They are rather felt. After proceeding to examine different artists' interpretations of Charles Dickens, Sir Walter Scott, George Eliot, and R. L. Stevenson, Chesterton demonstrates that, in every case, the artist cannot help but be a metaphysician with his or her portrait; this is because "every man's face in the street is a dark and perplexing allegory," again, a by-now familiar idea of Chesterton's.[43] This allegory (symbol) of the face is not a clear and beautiful window into the soul, but it is a dark and perplexing thing, not so much to be entirely apprehended as to be seen. We may not know what exactly this symbol yields until we experience it ourselves, and even then we will not so much gain a clear, metaphysical insight into

41. Chesterton, "Famous Novelists in the National Portrait Gallery," 1–8.
42. Chesterton, "Famous Novelists in the National Portrait Gallery," 2.
43. Chesterton, "Famous Novelists in the National Portrait Gallery," 4.

reality as a murky suggestion of sin or a bright suggestion of saintliness. In whichever instance, the symbol of the human face on the canvas is a revealer of that subject's soul, which is a fascinating, complex, and divine thing; "In portrait painting men's souls are mixed like paints on a palette, and produce such colours as were never seen in the most sensational sunset."[44]

In this article we see Chesterton, at the turn of the twentieth century, go well beyond the Ruskinian and, therefore, Victorian worship of beauty that, as we have seen, passed down to Pater and Wilde. Here Chesterton takes a turn for the grotesque, the irrational, and the symbolic. In short, Chesterton takes the symbolist turn. He writes that "ugliness is, in nine cases out of ten, much more worth drawing than beauty."[45]

So what precisely do these five early essays from *The Bookman* reveal about Chesterton's place as a critical conversation partner of Ruskin, Pater, and Wilde? Chesterton's symbolism, like that of W. B. Yeats, is a call for art to once again deal with humanity's deepest beliefs, as the myths, religions, and fables of old did. Similarly to Yeats, Chesterton often refers to "Fairyland" as that seemingly unreal realm which is actually more real than the life of the bourgeois businessman, dressed the same as everyone else, walking through the drab streets of London or Dublin. Fairyland reveals an imaginative power that is able to startle people and evoke the wonderful, deep truths of human existence. Unlike Ruskin, Pater, and Wilde, Chesterton is mostly unconcerned with beauty as an aesthetic *quality* of objects and landscapes. That is, he is not inclined to discuss aesthetics from a technical and philosophical standpoint. Rather, Chesterton concerns himself deeply with the way that aesthetic forms convey truth and reveal human worth. Chesterton echoes Yeats's concern that people have stripped the arts of their real and vital power by parsing the subject and meaning from pictures. I will return to Chesterton's relation to Yeats in a moment. First I want to mention some of Chesterton's other early journalistic activity related to art criticism. Along with the *Illustrated London News*, Chesterton wrote most often for the *Daily News*.

44. Chesterton, "Famous Novelists in the National Portrait Gallery," 4. The anthropocentrism in Chesterton's aesthetic is notably different to Ruskin's approach in *Modern Painters I* and *II* where we are the recipients, the beholders of beauty, not the objects of contemplation ourselves.

45. Chesterton, "Famous Novelists in the National Portrait Gallery," 4. Again, the difference between this view and Ruskin's is very apparent.

Chesterton began writing for the *Daily News* in 1901.[46] This periodical, the "leading Liberal newspaper" of England during the Edwardian era, which increased in circulation from eighty thousand in 1900 to four hundred thousand in 1909, was Chesterton's primary journalistic platform in the first decade of his career.[47] In such early articles as "The Mystery of the Mystics," "The Conundrum of Art," and "Art and the Churches" (which is an interesting review of P. T. Forsyth's book *Religion in Recent Art*),[48] Chesterton further demonstrates his agreement with Symons and the French symbolist authors.

In "Art and the Churches" from January 1902, Chesterton writes, "The first and most important thing about any man is his vision, or conception, of the universe."[49] After explaining how art cannot replace religion, he writes, "If we are content to live from henceforward upon the surface of things, never again to ask an absorbing question, or whisper a thrilling hypothesis, then indeed we may contrive to find a common ground in the sensuous pleasures of art."[50] Then, after naming artists such as Blake and Degas as well as the philosopher Schopenhauer, he admits that such figures could be enjoyed in some way purely on the surface. This is a backhanded way of making a concession to the aesthetes. "But the moment we went a little deeper, and began to feel that spirit, that moment the whole preposterous truce of modern culture would be shattered into pieces, and men would really be at each other's throats fighting for the honour of God or for the honour of the devil."[51] Chesterton is dismantling the aesthetes' position yet again; he is arguing that if one is a human being, then one cannot resist ideas, and one cannot but seek to penetrate to deeper truths behind an image.

In these and other early essays on artists, writers, and poets, we find that Chesterton was heavily engaged in symbolic exegesis of virtually everything. Even if not actively engaging with the writings of the French *symbolistes* (as his essay on Maeterlinck suggests), he at least was

46. Ker, *G. K. Chesterton*, 74.

47. Stapleton, *G. K. Chesterton at the Daily News*, "Columns, Reviews, and Letters, 1901–1902," xv, xx.

48. For an evaluation of Forsyth's theological aesthetics, see Pattison, *Art, Modernity, and Faith*.

49. Stapleton, *G. K. Chesterton at the Daily News*, 300.

50. Stapleton, *G. K. Chesterton at the Daily News*, 301.

51. Stapleton, *G. K. Chesterton at the Daily News*, 301.

intuitively sharing many of their sensibilities and echoing nearly all of their concerns.

Chesterton's Relation to Yeats

In discussing Chesterton as a symbolist, the other major point to be taken into consideration is Chesterton's friendship with his contemporary, the Irish poet and symbolist W. B. Yeats (1865–1939).[52] Chesterton's remarks on Yeats in the *Autobiography* are quite interesting, yet the importance of Chesterton and Yeats's friendship has been overlooked by contemporary scholars.[53] In the chapter "The Fantastic Suburb" of the *Autobiography* Chesterton reminisces about their friendship in the early years of the century: "I knew the family more or less as a whole in those days. . . . W. B. is perhaps the best talker I ever met, except his old father who alas will talk no more in this earthly tavern, though I hope he is still talking in Paradise."[54] Chesterton goes on to relate, "Yeats affected me strongly, but in two opposite ways; like the positive and negative poles of a magnet."[55] Yeats's strong effect on Chesterton happened in two ways; the positive was Yeats's symbolist imagination, the negative was his philosophy of idealism, that the physical world was a construct of pure mind. Chesterton says, "So that I found myself in this odd double attitude towards the poet, agreeing with him about the fairy-tales on which most people disagreed with him, and disagreeing with him about the philosophy on which most

52. A standard introduction to Yeats lays out his connection to the movement in question in this way: "Though Yeats later questioned a great many techniques of the French symbolists, . . . from first to last he seems to have accepted the basic symbolist proposition: the great symbol is not contained in the poem but is the poem itself: ultimately any work of art is 'an entire word.' The finished work of art stands for a feeling." And a few lines later the author writes, "Yeats, elaborating [the French symbolists'] ideas, sees the poem as a complex relationship of images, rhythms, and sounds which, in conjunction, become a symbol for emotional experiences otherwise inexpressible in words." From Unterecker, *A Reader's Guide to William Butler Yeats*, 30.

53. For example, Oddie mentions Yeats just once in his book on Chesterton's early development. Yet in the *Autobiography* Chesterton sees his relationship with Yeats (which began before the publication of *Orthodoxy*) as one of the most important friendships in his life. Throughout the chapter "The Fantastic Suburb" Chesterton muses on what they did together and on what matters they agreed or disagreed. See Chesterton, *Autobiography*, 133–55. There is more research to be done in this area of Yeats and Chesterton; I can only suggest some things in this chapter.

54. Chesterton, *Autobiography*, 142.

55. Chesterton, *Autobiography*, 143.

people agreed with him. . . ."[56] Whatever their exact philosophical disagreement, Yeats explains their commonly held conviction well: "Why should a man cease to be a scholar, a believer, a ritualist before he begins to paint or rhyme or to compose music . . . ?"[57] Here one can notice the reaction to the entire "art for art's sake" movement, a shaking of its foundations. Yeats, Chesterton, and other symbolists argued that, far from being incidental or damaging to artistic productions, one's own beliefs (in magic, the occult, Christianity, or whatever else) do not interfere with art. On the contrary, they actually nourish and enrich art. The fact is that the products of human creation are reflections of underlying ideas; paintings and compositions are visible manifestations of potent, unseen realities. The richer the ideas, the richer the creative production.

Could it be that Yeats's friendship as well as his essays and poetry informed Chesterton about the symbolist movement at a time when the young journalist was first discovering mysticism and Catholicism? Yeats's essay "William Blake and the Imagination" (1897) comes thirteen years before Chesterton's book on Blake, and Yeats's 1901 essay "Magic" finds a curious echo in Chesterton's play of 1913, *Magic*, subtitled *A Fantastic Comedy*.[58] Where Yeats infamously writes, "I believe in the practice and philosophy of what we have agreed to call magic, in what I must call the evocation of spirits, though I do not know what they are, in the power of creating magical illusions, in the visions of truth in the depths of the mind when the eyes are closed";[59] Chesterton replies by making his magician character, the Conjurer, say, "I don't wonder at your believing in fairies. As long as these things were my servants they seemed to me like fairies. When they tried to be my masters . . . I found they were not fairies. I found the spirits with whom I at least had come in contact were evil . . . awfully, unnaturally evil."[60]

Chesterton's symbolism, like that of W. B. Yeats, is a call for art to once again deal with humanity's deepest beliefs, as the myths, stories, folk tales, and fables of old did. Yeats and Chesterton both insist on the

56. Chesterton, *Autobiography*, 150. This is a key statement in Chesterton's autobiography; it was the symbolic, mythical fairy tales and folk tales, for example, from Yeats's popular books that Chesterton embraced. It was his religious and philosophical positions that Chesterton disagreed with and openly critiqued.

57. Graham and Hough, *Strangeness and Beauty*, 174.

58. Chesterton, *Magic: A Fantastic Comedy*.

59. Larrissy, *W. B. Yeats*, 344.

60. Chesterton, *Magic: A Fantastic Comedy*, 95.

primacy of the realm of the spirit, but Chesterton is ever wary of the evil spirits that he believed to be lurking there. Yeats and Chesterton both believe in magic, but Chesterton is ever recognizing the dangers of black magic. For both writers, "Fairyland" is that enchanted realm, more real than the drab, outward life that people live in the streets. For both writers, there is much to learn from the fairies—those secretive, human-like creatures living on the borderland, always reminding us of the magic underneath all things, ever surprising us, always reminding us how much more there is to the world than what the decadents and materialists think. Chesterton and Yeats are closely linked by time and friendship, but more importantly by their shared beliefs, approaches, and dispositions. The full range of this connection awaits a fuller treatment, but suffice it to say, we can situate Chesterton alongside the symbolists, especially via his friendship with Yeats; this will allow us to interpret his work as part of a much larger literary, artistic, and theosophical movement at the turn of the century.[61]

Chesterton's Book *G. F. Watts*

The first of Chesterton's two art books is about a painter largely overlooked today: G. F. Watts. The slim book simply titled *G. F. Watts* (1904)[62] is, after the popular *Robert Browning* (1903), one of Chesterton's first, book-length critical works. I wish to look at this particular work rather than the more famous *Heretics* (1905) or *Orthodoxy* (1908) for three reasons: firstly, it is from early in the century, and so was written during the years that Ruskin, Pater, Wilde, and Symons were widely read and enjoyed great popularity; secondly, like his other works, *G. F. Watts* is also primarily concerned with mystical, religious truths, yet it has not been mined as thoroughly as his spiritual autobiography *Orthodoxy*; thirdly, *G. F. Watts* is an examination of religion through a critical and *aesthetic*

61. Indeed, I believe this is where many biographies, popular studies, and introductions to Chesterton can mislead readers. While it is true that Chesterton was highly original, it is also true that he was enmeshed in the artistic and literary movements of Edwardian England during his formative, early years. He also was deeply involved in very many friendships and feuds in various circles of journalists, novelists, playwrights, and poets. Most of his writing is incidental, and so to obtain a full picture of Chesterton's range, one must also understand what he was supporting and what he was attacking. However, in his unique case, most of his enemies were also his closest friends.

62. Chesterton, *G. F. Watts*. Hereafter I cite this parenthetically as *Watts, #*.

lens rather than an autobiographical one (as in *Orthodoxy*) or a broadly philosophical-historical one (as in *The Everlasting Man*, first published in 1925).

Watts the artist is rather obscure in our current age. Picking up two recent works written on the Victorian artist, one finds in the introduction of each an honest estimation of the painter: "Of all the major players in the late-Victorian art world, George Frederic Watts (1817–1904) remains the most shadowy, elusive, quixotic, and yet the easiest to patronize or dismiss. . . . Watts is still a subterranean presence in most recent scholarly accounts of nineteenth-century British art."[63] In the other work we read, "At the time of his death in 1904 Watts was one of the most famous artists of his generation. There were obituaries in newspapers across the world. Today Watts provokes a mixed reaction and, for many, his name remains unknown."[64] Watts's art is deeply symbolic, and is frequently engaged with Greek mythology as well as the Bible. It is also characterized by religious feeling, for Watts wished to produce a kind of religious effect upon his audience. In *G. F. Watts: Victorian Visionary*, the artist is quoted as saying that his aim is "[that] art may speak . . . with the solemn and majestic ring in which the Hebrew prophet spoke to the Jews of old, demanding noble aspirations, [and] condemning . . . prevalent vices."[65] Watts was therefore concerned, like the symbolists, with uncovering truth through his symbolic vision, and not merely crafting a mood to charm or delight. In the following section I am utilizing the same interpretive framework I have used in my close reading of Ruskin, Pater, and Wilde, exploring the way that Chesterton interprets the relation between beauty and morality, truth, and religion. I argue in what follows that Chesterton's interpretation of Watts exhibits strong inclinations to a Catholic sacramentalism. In, with, and under the symbols that Watts has created, Chesterton is able to make discoveries, not of the abstract attributes of God, but of the hidden presence of God within mankind itself, a presence made manifest in acts of creativity. I will reiterate here that the terms "mysticism" and "allegory" are not technical terms in Chesterton's writings. The autodidact found mysticism and allegory beneath virtually all the paintings and poems he ever critiqued, and so we must understand these terms in the context of Chesterton. I shall demonstrate that for him, mysticism essentially

63. Trodd and Brown, *Representations of G. F. Watts*, 1.

64. Bills and Bryant, *G. F. Watts: Victorian Visionary*, xi.

65. Bills and Bryant, *G. F. Watts: Victorian Visionary*, 3.

means the hidden, spiritual center of humanity that can never be fully spoken of, and allegory has virtually the same meaning as symbol; to Chesterton, every outward form in art and literature, every brushstroke or word, is an outward, visible manifestation of inward, invisible truths.

Beauty & Morality in *G. F. Watts*

At the outset of *G. F. Watts*, Chesterton establishes the philosophical outlook of the great Victorian sages, among whom he considers Watts to be the final, and perhaps the greatest, example. Chesterton argues that the Victorians held a kind of "synthetic" philosophy; that is, whether in pulpit, poem, or painting, these creators never missed an opportunity to preach about the unity of all things in God (*Watts*, 18). Rather than chastising these Victorians for their moralizing, Chesterton simply commends their bravery in preaching as well as that synthesis of craft and message that they achieved. Chesterton shows that though Watts is a painter and not a philosopher or theologian, he is nevertheless a communicator of the "synthetic philosophy" of the age; he is one in whom the creative Spirit of God has emerged dramatically. Indeed, through his production of portraits and allegories, he has developed a "wonderful way of preaching, . . . he is certain that he is right" (*Watts*, 15). Therefore, Chesterton develops this picture of Watts as a giver of immortal truths to the public. Far from depicting obscure, esoteric doctrines through his allegorical pieces, Watts is actually creating approachable, democratic works that disclose eternal things. "For Watts' [*sic*] nature is essentially public, that is to say, it is modest and noble, and has nothing to hide" (*Watts*, 52).

Chesterton is ever concerned that art, religion, and mysticism should be accessible and democratic. In an essay from *The Daily News* titled "The Mystery of the Mystics" (August 30, 1901), Chesterton reviews a book on Christian mysticism but uses his column to give his own estimation of the democratic nature of true mystical experience. He writes, "Christian mysticism has by its very nature one seriously important difference from other mysticism—the fact that it is democratic, while all other mysticism tends to be aristocratic."[66] What does Chesterton mean by this? Perhaps that Christian mysticism is, like the art of Watts, democratic, accessible,

---

66. Stapleton, *G. K. Chesterton at the Daily News*, 173. For more on Chesterton's mysticism, see Wild, *The Tumbler of God: Chesterton as Mystic*.

revealed. The great revelation that the mystic, like Watts, has realized is that the world is filled with symbols: "It is the mystic to whom every star is like a sudden rocket, every flower an earthquake of the dust, who is the clear-minded man. Mysticism, or a sense of the mystery of things, is simply the most gigantic form of common sense."[67] Like Symons and the symbolists, Chesterton is re-evaluating mysticism and in so doing, he is offering a conception of religion in which faith rests on democratic and experiential grounds. Far from being something for secretive initiates, mysticism is actually for everyone. It is the intuitive sense of the mystery (for Chesterton, hiddenness, preciousness, sacredness) of all things. I will return to some of this later when I show how Chesterton explicitly connects Watts's moral intuition to democratic mysticism.

In a further exploration of the connections between art and morality in Watts's art, Chesterton, in a very revealing passage, writes of the Victorians: "Like Matthew Arnold, the last and most skeptical of them, who expressed their basic idea in its most detached and philosophic form, they held that conduct was three-fourths of life. They were ingrainedly ethical; the mere idea of thinking anything more important than ethics would have struck them as profane" (*Watts*, 69). Chesterton is intent on demonstrating that when it comes to this foundation of both society and the arts, morality, Watts is cut from the same moral cloth as the Victorian sages. The passage continues, "The mere thought of Watts painting a picture called *The Victory of Joy over Morality*, or *Nature rebuking Conscience*, is enough to show the definite limits of that cosmic equality. . . . He simply draws the line somewhere, as all men, including anarchists draw it somewhere; his is dogmatic as all sane men are dogmatic" (*Watts*, 70). Watts has definite ideas (dogmas) about the world, and his art is greater, broader, and more important because of its reflection of these ideas. This symbolism is not a shallow didacticism that Watts lords over his spectators, but a thoroughly dogmatic, mystical vision.

So far Chesterton interprets Watts's art as accessible, democratic, and deeply moral. Yet Chesterton fundamentally differs from his critical predecessors, particularly Ruskin, in his estimation of didacticism in art. Weaving a path between Ruskin, who stated that art *always* teaches, and the aesthetes, who believed art must *never* teach, Chesterton argues that art is *unable* to teach. The passage is worth quoting:

<hr>

67. Stapleton, *G. K. Chesterton at the Daily News*, 173.

> About the whole of this Watts controversy about didactic art
> there is at least one perfectly plain and preliminary thing to be
> said. It is said that art cannot teach a lesson. This is true, and the
> only proper addition is the statement that neither, for the matter
> of that, can morality teach a lesson. For a thing to be didactic, in
> the strict and narrow and scholastic sense, it must be something
> about facts or the physical sciences: you can only teach a lesson
> about such a thing as Euclid or the making of paper boats . . .
> A picture cannot give a plain lesson in morals; neither can a
> sermon. A didactic poem was a thing known indeed among the
> ancients and the old Latin civilization, but as a matter of fact it
> scarcely ever professed to teach people how to live the higher
> life. It taught people how to keep bees. (*Watts*, 120–21)

This passage is highly illustrative of both Chesterton's humor and his symbolist path. His point is that didacticism is always impossible in art (painting, speech—even sermons!) unless a product is created from the beginning with the intention of teaching practical lessons, such as how to keep bees. Then it is no longer a painted picture, as Chesterton refers to it, but something else. Euclid, paper boats, and beekeeping are Chesterton's examples of things for which didactic lessons exist. These are not in the realm of art but of education, of course. A painting cannot directly teach a lesson; this is impossible by its very nature. Rather, art presents to the beholder something unseen or eternal which it does not "teach," but suggests, outlines, uncovers.

For Chesterton, then, art democratically presents a kind of mysticism, an intuitive response through which deeper things may be grasped. We must remember that the didactic system of Ruskin said that art is an interpreter of truths about God gathered from nature, that it can teach, instruct, and shape hearts. Ruskin's theoria considers natural phenomena to point to the ordered attributes of a Creator. As we have seen, Ruskin is then able to link landscape art to the truths of landscapes themselves. In his system, creation communicates the attributes of God, which are always true, clear, and discernible in natural phenomena such as trees, mountains, minerals, etc. Landscape art is therefore the commentary on all such divinely authored phenomena. Ruskin then insists that art must be as clear, as accurate, as faithful as possible.

Chesterton's view of art is certainly different: "Since we find, therefore, that ethics is like art, a mystic and intuitional affair, the only question that remains is, have they any kinship" (*Watts*, 121). Though Chesterton does share Ruskin's insistence that all art is moral, he does not share Ruskin's other conclusions. Art does not need rules; it does not always need to be balanced; it does not even need to be "accurate." In Chesterton's view, if a painting somehow leads a viewer to deeper, spiritual realities via its symbols, then such a painting is true art.

Chesterton begins to answer the question of kinship between art and ethics when he writes, "If they have not, a man is not a man, but two men and probably more: if they have, there is, to say the least of it, at any rate a reasonable possibility that a note in moral feeling might have affinity with a note in art" (*Watts*, 121). An artist cannot help but convey some moral feeling in art, which means an artist cannot help but symbolize. Art is not able to not symbolize; for every artist's activity is a "mystical and intuitional affair."

This is far from meaning that all art is somehow tainted by artists' beliefs. In *G. F. Watts*, the aesthetes are the targets: "But the meanings expressed in high and delicate art are not to be classed under cheap and external ethical formulae, they deal with strange vices and stranger virtues. Art is only unmoral in so far as most morality is immoral" (*Watts*, 122). Ruskin would be hesitant to engage in such a dangerous paradox. Chesterton is not contradicting himself here but is pointing out that things are not always what they purport to be. A complex painting, such as one of Watts's, does not have a "simple" message, as if one could sum it up in a few words and include every possible meaning. Each painting is a little world, an immense yet hidden mystery, incapable of being simplistically summarized. Art is only unmoral when it is like shallow morality, when it deals only in surface illusions and tricks, empty rules and formulae. Real art for Chesterton is like real morality, something immense, strong, and human. Therefore, a truly great work does stir up, in a mysterious way, these "strange vices and stranger virtues," which the viewer cannot "pick up" by a quick look at the painting, but will slowly come to see while contemplating its mystery.

Beauty & Truth in *G. F. Watts*

G. F. Watts' rich, allegorical paintings fascinated Chesterton, and in his book Chesterton seeks to uncover the mystery of these allegorical paintings for the reader. He argues that allegories unlock deeper truths, but they do not provide a simplistic key for the disclosure of the whole truth. That is, allegorical paintings do not contribute to a picture of a truth that underlies every system, as in Ruskin. Neither do allegories turn a piece of art into a moral or didactic tool, nullifying its beauty and delight, as Pater and Wilde argued. Chesterton discards Ruskin's system yet believes in his God. Then he also discards the aesthetes' agnosticism yet believes in their position regarding the immense, godlike power of human imagination and creativity.

Because Watts's art is so allegorical, it is continually revealing mysterious truths *through* figures and scenes. Chesterton's interpretation of Watts's art connects it to the unveiling of these truths again and again. In an important sentence, Chesterton makes the argument that whether the path be painting, literature, or philosophy, each is attempting to express central truths of humanity's existence: "Watts is not a man copying literature or philosophy, but rather a man copying the great spiritual and central realities which literature and philosophy also set out to copy" (*Watts*, 115). Rather than denigrating Watts's art, Chesterton praises it when he refers to it as "copying." For this is neither a slavish copying of nature nor a shallow copying of others' styles; it is rather a symbolizing of mystical truths that lie at the bottom of all human experience. In a brilliant interpretation of what is perhaps Watts's most recognizable work, *Hope* (1886), Chesterton gives us further insight into his theory of allegory in art.

The argument is that all art is allegorical, and since language is an art, it must also be so: "For the truth is, that language is not a scientific thing at all, but wholly an artistic thing, a thing invented by hunters, and killers, and such artists, long before science was dreamed of" (*Watts*, 91). All human creation then symbolizes the strivings, urges, passions, and beliefs of the humans who set out to engage with the "great spiritual and central realities" mentioned above. In fact, even language is an artistic creation, and those hunters or killers who created it did so as artists.[68] Art precedes science, temporally, symbolically, and spiritually. Far from being the finely tuned, artificial creations of scientists, words come from artists engaged in basic and deeply human pursuits.

In Chesterton's highly symbolic world, each word or artefact points beyond itself to elementary truths. For him, then, both the word "hope" and the Watts painting that is named "Hope" are highly charged symbols.

---

68. Chesterton had a fascination with the artistic creativity of primitive mankind, a creativity that preceded any notion of modern science by many thousands of years. Much later, in his work *The Everlasting Man*, Chesterton will marvel at the cave art of Lascaux, pointing out the human creativity in such colorful depictions of animals. See Chesterton, *The Everlasting Man*, 29–32.

Chesterton writes, "It represents a certain definite thing, the word 'hope.' But what does the word 'hope' represent? It represents only a broken instantaneous glimpse of something that is immeasurably older and wilder than language, that is immeasurably older and wilder than man; a mystery to saints and a reality to wolves" (*Watts*, 96–97). Chesterton still has not explicitly answered his question, but now we know that hope is real, mysterious, and ancient. Watts's painting is, like the word hope itself, a symbol for a great truth:

> He would see something for which there is neither speech nor language, which has been too vast for any eye to see and too secret for any religion to utter, even as an esoteric doctrine. Standing before that picture he finds himself in the presence of a great truth. He perceives that there is something in man which is always apparently on the eve of disappearing, but never disappears, an assurance which is always apparently saying farewell and yet illimitably lingers, a string which is always stretched to snapping and yet never snaps. (*Watts*, 98)

The great truth, Chesterton goes on to explain, is that hope is faith that survives; it is "a perpetually defeated thing which survives all its conquerors" (*Watts*, 101). The word or the image of hope—this symbol—reveals this truth: "But the point is that this title is not (as those think who call it 'literary') the reality behind the symbol, but another symbol for the same thing, or to speak yet more strictly, another symbol describing another part or aspect of the same complex reality" (*Watts*, 101–2). Chesterton writes about truth as a complex, multifaceted reality that may be revealed in one way or another. Yet, it is vast and secret, and so cannot be ever fully and systematically explained, simply hinted at by words or by images. The mode does not necessarily matter to Chesterton, as if he thought one medium to be higher than another; he does not rank the arts as some nineteenth-century philosophers and Oscar Wilde were wont to do. For Watts's paintings demonstrate that some truths need both words and images to be hinted at, let alone grasped by the heart; words and images work in tandem to uncover hidden truths.

G. F. Watts is the earliest and fullest treatment of aesthetic ideas in G. K. Chesterton's *oeuvre*. Chesterton's symbolist answer to Ruskin, Pater, and Wilde posits the definite existence of truths, but asserts they are vast; secrets that can merely be hinted at. The goal of artistic production is also the goal of artistic criticism, and that goal is not to form a comprehensive system nor to achieve an exquisite mood. Art and art criticism open us up to the experience of truths unveiling themselves. Such truths are like mysterious riddles to be played with and just as playfully retold and enjoyed again. The artist may not be aware of the symbolism she or he employs in the creation of a riddle, and here is where the importance of the critic—especially of Chesterton the critic—comes in.

Beauty & God in *G. F. Watts*

Watts presents a harmony of Athens and Jerusalem, of chiseled pagan beauty and multilayered Christian symbolism. In this combination he represents the modern movement of symbolism: "His art is an out-door art, like that of the healthy ages of the world, like the statuesque art of Greece, like the ecclesiastical and external Gothic art of Christianity: an art that can look the sun in the face" (*Watts*, 52–53). Not only do Watts's paintings broadly appeal to people because of their wide variety of subject matter, but his paintings share the characteristic of a timeless, eternal style. Chesterton notes that in Watts's art, there are never any ecclesiastical or civic symbols; indeed, in Watts's so-called allegorical paintings, there is even a noticeable lack of recognizable personages, either biblical or literary. There is nothing to connect his art to historical events. Instead, "a primeval vagueness and archaism hangs over all the canvases and cartoons, like frescoes from some prehistoric temple. There is nothing but the eternal things, clay and fire and the sea, and motherhood and the dead" (*Watts*, 59). Watts captures the "eternal things" and the things coming from the "palette of Creation" in his art. There is nothing in his content or his style that binds him to fads or fancies of his age. He is, in Chesterton's mind, a painter at the height of his divinely gifted powers: "A curious lustre or glitter, conveyed chiefly by a singular and individual brush-work, lies over all his great pictures. It is the dawn of things: it is the glow of the primal sense of wonder; it is the sun of the childhood of the world" (*Watts*, 133). Notice the connections Chesterton readily makes between the qualities of Watts's technique and color with true perception itself, described as "wonder" and "childhood." Chesterton continues on this theme of glowing sun: "[I]t is the light that never was on sea or land; but still it is a light shining on things, not shining through them. It is a light which exhibits and does honour to this world, not a light that breaks in upon this world to bring it terror or comfort" (*Watts*, 133). Watts is thus an artist of this time, this world, this reality. In his work he somehow is able to channel the vital energy of creation at the primal dawn of things. He has divine-like powers. Chesterton is capable of lofty praise not because he idolizes Watts or even thinks he is the most talented of artists. Watts's art exemplifies the God-given, creative talents of humanity, and so has revealed something of the awesome gift that artists have received.

Chesterton is therefore ever willing to compare and then credit the creativity of Watts to the creativity of God. Regarding Watts's keen use of color, Chesterton writes, "So individual is his handling that his very choice and scale of colours betrays him. A man with a keen sense of the spiritual and symbolic history of colours could guess at something about Watts from the mess on his palette. He would see giants and the sea and cold primeval dawns and brown earthmen and red earth-women lying in the heaps of greens and whites and reds, like forces in chaos before the first day of creation" (*Watts*, 126). Chesterton interprets Watts as such a person who has been given this "spiritual and symbolic history of colours," as he boldly advances his personal interpretations of several works. He continues to guide the reader, demonstrating where and why Watts commands colors like God commands the elements. Noting that certain colors appear in Watts's paintings like they do nowhere else, Chesterton writes, "Then there is that tremendous autochthonous red, which was the color of Adam, whose name was Red Earth. It is, if one may say so, the clay in which no one works, except Watts and the Eternal Potter" (*Watts*, 129).

Chesterton maintains this tone throughout his discussion: "There are other colours that have this character, a character indescribable except by saying that they come from the palette of Creation—a green especially that reappears through portraits, allegories, landscapes, heroic designs, but always has the same fierce and elfish look, like a green that has a secret" (*Watts*, 129). Chesterton goes on, "But all these colours have, as I say, the first and most characteristic and most obvious of the mental qualities of Watts; they are simple and like things just made by God" (*Watts*, 129). Where Ruskin compares the attributes of God to the assorted colors on a canvas, and then tests for the artist's "accuracy" and "fidelity" to God's works, Chesterton compares the choice of colors on a canvas to the choices of God in creation. He looks at the human artist as a small version of God himself. The difference may seem subtle, but it is immensely important. Yet, Chesterton's rhetoric might appear to get out of hand here. Does Watts work as God works? Can any artist have such command over colors so as to mirror the Divine Creator? Is the human individual simultaneously a work of art and an artist of work; that is, a creation that can also create?

The book answers all these questions in the affirmative. The *imago Dei* reality of each man and each woman is well demonstrated through Watts's gift for painting—surprisingly—people's backs. In what is, perhaps, the most important passage in the book, Chesterton argues that hardly any other artist throughout history has had such an obsession, with the exception of Moses; Moses caught a fleeting glimpse of God's glory when God permitted him to only see his back (*Watts*, 139). This is recorded in Exodus and is one of Chesterton's many biblical allusions in discussing Watts's work.[69] In making this comparison, Chesterton is saying that Watts, too, sees the presence or glory of God in the backs of the figures he paints, most often in his allegorical works such as "Dawn" (*Watts*, 131), "Eve Repentant" (*Watts*, 137), and "Love and Death" (*Watts*, 141). In his portraits Watts thus "makes [people] over again," and when he endeavors to depict a man or woman, that is, a being made in the very image of the Creator of the Universe, Watts therefore "dips his hand in the clay of chaos" and re-creates the person he paints (*Watts*, 145).

Chesterton's language would be considered outrageous according to the system of theoria and the mode of aesthesis. But for Chesterton there can be no possible alternative; if each sitter whose likeness Watts paints is made in the image of God, then Watts (who is also in the image of God) cannot but step into a divine role when he lays the brush upon his canvas to begin a portrait. This is the heart of Chesterton's theological aesthetic and the most original part of his contribution to this conversation—or battle—over religion and aesthetics at the turn of the century. For Watts "the hero, the great man, was a man more human than humanity itself. In worshipping him you were worshipping humanity in a sacrament: and Watts seems to express in almost every line of his brush this ardent and reverent view of the great man. He overdoes it" (*Watts*, 149). Then a few pages later he explicitly states that Watts saw the image of God in his sitters where modern artists do not even see "the image of man" (*Watts*, 157).[70] This is Chesterton's interpretation: in his ability to see that Divine

---

69. The Bible reference is this: "'But,' he said, 'you cannot see my face, for man shall not see me and live.'" And the Lord said, "'Behold, there is a place by me where you shall stand on the rock, and while my glory passes by I will put you in a cleft of the rock, and I will cover you with my hand until I have passed by. Then I will take away my hand, and you shall see my back, but my face shall not be seen'" (Exod 33:20–23).

70. Later critiquing Aubrey Beardsley's depiction of women, Chesterton will write,

image in his sitters, Watts is doing something deeply theological through the use of symbols, even if he is doing this unknowingly. Watts re-tells or even re-performs the story of God's creation through his art, and he steps into a God-like role by bringing out this divinity residing within each of his sitters. In this act Watts is not only a deeply moral artist, but a deeply theological one.

Chesterton brings his work to a close by commenting again upon Watts's human and therefore paradoxically, divine powers; it is he who, "Standing before a dark canvas upon some quiet evening, has made lines and something has happened. In such an hour the strange and splendid phrase of the Psalm he has literally fulfilled. He has gone on because of the word of meekness and truth and of righteousness. And his right hand has taught him terrible things" (*Watts*, 169). This paraphrase of Psalm 45:4 gives a final, biblical touch to a criticism of such an artist who, in Chesterton's mind, is not only the very image of the Creator, like any human, but has the creative powers to illustrate and celebrate this fact of existence. This is more than rhetorical praise; Chesterton considers the "art for art's sake" aesthetic to be silly and impossible. When a painting is a painting, it *always* deals with primordial truths; the creative power of artists demonstrates the mark of God within them.

In all of this Chesterton gives a picture of the artist that does not exactly fit Ruskin's view or Pater and Wilde's view. For Ruskin, a painter like J. M. W. Turner had the ability to comment upon nature-scripture; the oracles of God have been given to the artist to contemplate and then interpret for all others. Art then points to God's traits in some way. In Ruskin, the artist himself or herself is a prophet, a great communicator, and a critic is this prophet's scribe. Then, we have seen that Pater and Wilde believe that artistic works, with their charming colors and beauty, have no deeper meaning than what is found on the surface. Artists therefore have a kind of hieratic power to provide salvation by giving us such exquisite images, and the critic's role is to cut through moral and meta-physical distractions in presenting such work to the public.

So, we have these two Victorian views of the artist: as prophet, to re-present creation so it might help us see and understand God, and as priest, to perform beautiful and therefore salvific acts. Chesterton takes these two views and, through his discovery of each person's uniqueness,

---

"Now the queer females of Aubrey Beardsley are queerest of all in this, that they are not even female. They are narrow where women have a curve and cropped where women have a head of hair." See *William Blake*, 192.

that is, his or her *imago Dei* essence, unveils the creativity of God through the creativity of a painter. Watts is neither just a prophet nor a priest: he is a creator, making meaningful symbols in an analogous way to God. And Chesterton, as a critic, does not explain away these symbols with words, but he uncovers through his prose the same eternal truths and realities Watts uncovered through his paint. In his elevated praise of the power of artists, Chesterton does not quite fit Ruskin's system nor Pater's mold; he instead forges his own path, a path that seeks to recover the old system. It is a symbolist path that leads closer and closer to the role of Jesus Christ and the truth of Christianity.

In the next part of this chapter, I argue that Chesterton takes his position a step further to an even more overtly theological position. For it is in *William Blake* that Chesterton introduces the centrality of the incarnation into his theological aesthetic; Chesterton argues that Blake's genius is in his artistic depiction of the tangible and fleshly reality of Christ. He who is fully God yet also fully human will raise humanity up to divinity.

Chesterton's *William Blake*

This slim book on Blake is part of the same series as *G. F. Watts* (1904) and is the only other full volume Chesterton wrote on an individual painter.[71] Published in 1910, *William Blake* concerns not only Blake's visual art, but his life, poetry, and mysticism. Like *G. F. Watts*, this book helps us to see how Chesterton recovered the Catholic and mystical tradition in the wake of the aesthetic movements contending with one another at the *fin de siècle*. In the book he resolves the aesthetic tensions of art for art's sake, impressionism, and decadence into a symbolist answer, arguing that Blake's technique and vision stemmed from his supernaturalism. Blake's overall posture toward the cosmos is Chesterton's overriding emphasis in this book, and he demonstrates how Blake's very fine and chiseled artistic technique symbolizes the definiteness of the Deity as incarnated in the fully divine and fully human Jesus.

---

71. Chesterton, *William Blake*. Hereafter I cite this in the text as (*Blake*, page #). The series was The Popular Library of Art, with volumes on artists from Holbein to Whistler. Ford Madox Ford was also a contributor, writing the volumes on Rossetti and the Pre-Raphaelites. Chesterton did write other critical works on nineteenth-century figures, but only these two books on artists. His many other critical works dealt with novelists, poets, art critics, etc., especially Browning, Dickens, Pater, Wilde, Whistler, and Shaw.

Chesterton writes about Blake's "matured and massive supernaturalism" that is reflected in style and content in every poem, picture, and prophecy (*Blake*, 9). The overriding argument is that in Blake's work there is a continual obsession with "the eternal images of things," that is, the eternal *imago Dei* made visible in each person as artist (*Blake*, 160). In Blake's work there is this strong message of a knowable, visible, definite Deity. For Blake believes (as does Chesterton) that since God imprints himself into his creatures, his creatures may embody him. The incarnation of God, or the embodiment of God as a human himself, is the central tenet of Blake's mystical belief system, and, as Chesterton will argue, the central element of all of Blake's art.

Beauty & Morality in *William Blake*

The relation of beauty to morality is an interesting one in Blake because he seems to push the boundaries of conventional morality. This is often seen as problematic for Christian interpreters. Blake was prone to ecstatic visions, mystical experiences, bizarre activities, and violent, even abusive, outbursts against friends and enemies alike (*Blake*, 29). It is true that Blake was not the sort of public moralist or preacher that Ruskin, Watts, and some later Victorians were, in Chesterton's estimation. Blake did not paint on large canvases, nor did he execute enormous commissions in order to reach as many people as possible; rather, his art was often small and private, and many of his illustrated books were printed in surprisingly small quantities.[72] Blake's activities were different because his intentions were different. While Blake could achieve the greatest expressions of truth, beauty, and goodness—for the sake of the art itself—he was also capable of lies, heresies, and follies, at least according to Chesterton. For all the great beauty in Blake's creations, there was also great ugliness in other creations. Chesterton holds up as an example the picture titled, "The Man Who Built the Pyramids" (1819). It is this somewhat strange picture that convinced Chesterton of Blake's capacity for utter foolishness: "I think it is impossible to look at some of the pictures which Blake drew, under what he considered direct spiritual dictation, without feeling that he was from time to time under influences that were not only evil but even foolishly evil" (*Blake*, 100). Chesterton goes on to explain that

---

72. Blake's only book to achieve even limited sales during his lifetime was *Songs of Innocence and of Experience*; see Blake, *The Complete Illuminated Books*, 42.

Blake claimed to have conversed with this man's spirit, and then he goes on to describe the drawing, which is a side profile of the "face of an evil idiot, a leering, half-witted face with no chin and the protuberant nose of a pig" (*Blake*, 101). This "demoniac silliness" left Blake "sillier than it found him" (*Blake*, 101).

Blake's art corresponds to his beliefs. Yet despite his strangeness, his art was never foul or base; it was obscure, foolish even, but never completely immoral. This is because Blake's overriding concern was to picture God, a definite and personal God. Chesterton writes that all his follies were inherited from the eighteenth century, the age that "was primarily the release (as its leaders held) of reason and nature from the control of the Church" (*Blake*, 123). This century, with its popular mystics and magicians, "was not the release of the natural, but also of the supernatural, and also, alas! Of the unnatural. The heathen mystics hidden for two thousand years came out of their caverns . . ." (*Blake*, 123). Blake was a product of this time and was caught up in the teachings of Cagliostro and Swedenborg. Yet, according to Chesterton, Blake's genius and message absolve him from his religious mistakes. As Chesterton writes, "These things Blake did inherit from that break up of belief that can be called the eighteenth century: we will debit him with these as an inheritance. And when we have said this we have said everything that can be said of any debt he owed. His debts are cleared here. His estate is cleared with this payment. All that follows is himself" (*Blake*, 125–26). Chesterton decides that, rather than form the total picture of who Blake is, these eighteenth-century esoteric figures should be interpreted as influencing the artist only at his weaker moments. Blake was too strong and too much a genius to be led astray from his "massive supernaturalism." This massive supernaturalism, this ability to see the very outline of God, is Blake's curious contribution to both the history of art and to theological aesthetics. For him the importance of art was not in communicating Divine attributes that might be proclaimed by nature. It was also not in experiencing rapturous beauty that approaches or becomes religious experience. The importance of art for Blake was in its potential to lay bare the truths of God, humanity, and the cosmos. This he did in his singular fusion of the engraved and written line, melding the image and word in his radically unique compositions.

There are (at least) two types of artists in Chesterton's estimation: the *specialist* and the *universalist*. Blake was a universalist like few other artists of his time were. One of Chesterton's most important discussions in the study of Blake concerns his controversy with the artist Thomas Sto-thard. A wealthy patron, R. H. Cromek, had commissioned Stothard to paint a scene of Chaucer's Canterbury pilgrims after he had already asked for it from Blake. In a mean trick he then accepted Stothard's painting and rejected Blake's (*Blake*, 50). Although this episode does reveal important biographical information about Blake's frustrating relationship with his patrons, Chesterton sees this controversy as symbolic of a much greater struggle. This is the eternal struggle in art between the "specialist" and the "universalist."[73] Stothard was a specialist; from a technical standpoint his art is much more finely executed than Blake's. He achieves an accuracy that Blake never achieves. Yet, he is the lesser artist compared to Blake because art is more than fidelity to nature or the emphasis of beauty; it is an *apocalypse*, an unveiling of true things. Those specialists who perfect their artistic technique above all else sacrifice something very great. Only the truly great artists such as Da Vinci and Michelangelo understand "the subject as well as the picture" (*Blake*, 60).

This understanding is not technical knowledge, but poetic knowl-edge. The greatest artists are also the greatest poets, which means their conception of the world is grounded in their knowledge of the truth; from this they are able to draw out the essences of things (*Blake*, 101). This poetic art is necessarily courageous and honest, because it communicates a true, moral image. Chesterton writes, "But the truth is that unless art is moral, art is not only immoral, but immoral in the most commonplace, slangy, and prosaic way. In the future, the fastidious artists will go down to history as the embodiment of all the vulgarities and banalities of their time" (*Blake*, 63). The views, opinions, and morals of an artist are left per-manently imprinted in his or her work. Therefore, an artist like Stothard who does not grasp Chaucer will only be able to paint an aesthetically fine picture of Chaucer's characters. Stothard may understand his craft, but he does not understand the subject. So, such a picture will ultimately be shallow, dishonest, and immoral. Blake's greatness lies not in his ac-curacy or fidelity to nature, but in his understanding of things, most importantly of humanity and God. His pictures imaginatively reveal the eternity that lies at the essence of all things, especially within the artist himself. Chesterton will develop this further.

73. Chesterton first introduces these terms to describe Briton Riviere. See Chester-ton, "Literary Pictures of the Year: I—Shakespeare, Tennyson, Dickens," 79–84.

Beauty & Truth in *William Blake*

Chesterton thinks that Blake's firm, fixed line is the chief quality of his work (*Blake*, 17). As he has explained in *G. F. Watts*, no artist made in God's image can avoid demonstrating some approach to reality in her or his style. Thus, the key to Blake's philosophy is in his unique style: "No one can understand Blake's pictures, no one can understand a hundred allusions in his epigrams, satires, and art criticism who does not first of all realise that William Blake was a fanatic on the subject of the firm line" (*Blake*, 17). This follows a discussion of Blake's teacher, John Flaxman, who was "known for classicism at its clearest and coldest" (*Blake*, 16). Blake was thus an artist raised in the spirit of Greece, with its definite lines, flat perspective, and glorifying of the body. "The thing he loved most in art was that lucidity and decision of outline which can be seen best in the cartoons of Raphael, in the Elgin Marbles, and in the simpler designs of Michael Angelo. The thing he hated most in art was the thing which we now call Impressionism—the substitution of atmosphere for shape, the sacrifice of form to tint, the cloudland of the mere colourist" (*Blake*, 17–18). Clear form, solid shape, fixed line—Chesterton insists that Blake is interested in real things. Blake's style thus corresponds to fixed, objective reality, not the charming dreamland that Chesterton thinks impressionism is. "[Blake] loved to think that even in being a draughtsman he was also a sculptor. When he put his lines on a decorative page he would have much preferred to carve them out of marble or cut them into rock. Like every true romantic, he loved the irrevocable" (*Blake*, 21). Such a hard and final conception of figures, from Job to Satan, shows that Blake was not lacking in courage, for, "No coward could have drawn such pictures" (*Blake*, 22). Blake's pictures are *true* in the sense that they express the true hardness, materiality, and reality of people and things. His art is never suggestive because it is never timid; "The figure of man may be a monster, but he is a solid monster. The figure of God may be a mistake but it is an unmistakable mistake" (*Blake*, 23). Blake goes so far to depict a physical, circumscribed God. I will return to Blake's conception of the tangibility and solidity of God below. For now, I want to focus upon Chesterton's estimation of Blake as a philosophical realist.

Blake's solid design is the key to understanding his realism and celebration of materiality. "For the highest dogma of the spiritual is to affirm the material" (*Blake*, 135); this is a key idea for Chesterton. Blake was not a materialist, accepting the existence of *only* the material, observable, temporal realm, and neither was he an impressionist, rejecting essential truths for surface-level impressions; he was a *realist*. Chesterton makes a distinction from the realist of today who is merely a person who "begins at the outside of a thing: sometimes merely at the end of a thing" (*Blake*, 136). Instead, Chesterton believes, Blake shares many of the same beliefs as the realists of the Middle Ages; "In the twelfth century a Realist meant exactly the opposite; it meant a man who began at the inside of a thing" (*Blake*, 136). Such a man is Blake.

Further explaining his view of Blake's philosophical outlook, Chesterton points out, "All his animals are as absolute as the animals on a shield of heraldry" (*Blake*, 136), and then encourages the reader to test this characteristic interpretation for him- or herself. "[G]o back and read William Blake's poems about animals, as, for instance, about the lamb and about the tiger. You will see quite clearly that he is talking of an eternal tiger, who rages and rejoices forever in the sight of God. You will see that he is talking of an eternal and supernatural lamb, who can only feed happily in the fields of heaven" (*Blake*, 137). The truth of Blake's art is not the truth of Turner's art as Ruskin defended it. For Blake's animals are not anatomically correct; his trees are not drawn *en plein air*; his stars, mountains, and hills look too exaggerated to be accurate to nature. Yet this is not a problem for Blake and especially not for Chesterton, because the artist has the freedom to create observationally or scientifically inaccurate things, if these things unveil something more deeply true than what lies on the surface. It is the artist's God-given prerogative to be creative in this way.

In an interesting passage on the brilliant *fin-de-siècle* artist Aubrey Beardsley, Chesterton discusses Blake's exaggeration in relation to truth. In one of the most important passages of the book, Chesterton writes,

> Blake's work may be fantastic; but it is a fantasia on an old and recognisable air. It exaggerates characteristics. Blake's women are too womanish, his young men are too athletic, his old men are too preposterously old. But Aubrey Beardsley does not really exaggerate; he understates. His young men have less than the energy of youth. His women fascinate by the weakness of sex rather than by its strength. In short, one must have some truth to exaggerate.[74]

74. Chesterton, *Blake*, 195.

Such a passage would be abhorrent to Ruskin who insisted on measured, pure, and ideal beauty in all things, from landscapes to the human figure.[75] Indeed, Chesterton's delight in exaggeration could not be farther from Ruskin's view, as he outlines in *Modern Painters II*. Ruskin writes that every school of art should have one word "relieved out in deep letters of pure gold,—Moderation."[76] Yet Chesterton is not following Ruskin's theoretic faculty with its distinction between vital and typical beauty, its rejection of the exaggerated or crude, and its call for measured restraint. Chesterton is more akin to Pater and Wilde just here in their taste for the strange and the exaggerated. Wilde writes, "Where there is no exaggeration there is no love,"[77] and Chesterton wholeheartedly agrees, though with this crucial caveat: there is *true* exaggeration and there is *false* exaggeration. Chesterton writes, "The decadent mystic produces an effect not by exaggerating but by distorting. True exaggeration is a thing both subtle and austere. Caricature is a serious thing; it is almost blasphemously serious. Caricature really means making a pig more like a pig than even God has made him" (*Blake*, 195).

Coming from a talented caricaturist, this "philosophy of caricature" is further enlightening. Chesterton's caricatures are frequently brilliant, expressive, and exaggerative, as one might expect from reading such remarks on Blake.[78] Fifteen years after writing *William Blake* and following his conversion to Roman Catholicism, Chesterton would write in the seventh chapter in his biography on Aquinas, "If things deceive us, it is by being more real than they seem. As ends in themselves they always deceive us; but as things tending to a greater end, they are even more real than we think them."[79] For Chesterton, Blake's art presented exag-

---

75. For example, see Ruskin, MP II, 126: "Which orderly balance and arrangement are essential to the perfect operation of the more earnest and solemn qualities of the Beautiful, as being heavenly in their nature, and contrary to the violence and disorganization of sin. . . ." See also MP II, 139: "But the least appearance of violence or extravagance, of the want of moderation and restraint, is, I think, destructive of all beauty whatsoever in everything, colour, form, motion, language, or thought. . . ." Ruskin also reacts strongly against "that lower host of things brilliant, magnificent, and redundant," and even more strongly against "the loose, the lawless, the exaggerated, the insolent, and the profane . . ." (MP II, 140).

76. Ruskin, MP II, 141.

77. Warner and Hough, *Strangeness and Beauty*, 2:141.

78. See Dale, *The Art of G. K. Chesterton*, 99–101. Also see Chesterton, *The Colored Lands*.

79. Chesterton, *St Thomas Aquinas—St. Francis of Assisi*, 164–65.

gerated forms of animals, people, and God that, rather than create a false picture, imaginatively uncovered the fact that "they are even more real than we think them." God and his creatures are strange beings, filled with divine energy, that ordinary people have become too accustomed to. It is only by art that shocks the system, such as Blake's, that we learn to see rightly again.

Beauty & God in *William Blake*

Blake's universality and his classical influences root him simultaneously in two eras. Like Watts, Blake's imagination was also a fusion of the classical and medieval, of the natural (material) and supernatural. In this fusion Chesterton sees a kind of paganism raising its head throughout different epochs. Blake is an inheritor of this paganism, which Chesterton calls "paganism in the original and frightful forest sense—pagan magic, . . . black magic" (*Blake*, 120). Chesterton continues, "The point is that this non-Christian supernaturalism, whether it was good or bad, was continuous in spite of Christianity. Its signs and traces can be seen in every age . . ." (*Blake*, 120). Then Chesterton traces this pagan supernaturalism from the dying Roman Empire through Gnosticism in the ancient church, to the Templars of the Middle Ages, then to the sixteenth-century Reformers, and eventually leading to the eighteenth century's Swedenborgianism. Blake inherits this supernatural paganism, as Chesterton calls it, and it melds with the other influences in his life. What results causes some confusion because it is difficult to pin down exactly what (or who) led Blake to his own mystical conclusions. In an interesting work from 1948, *The Theology of William Blake*, J. G. Davies has pointed out that through the years critics have held very different opinions on Blake's religious mysticism; is he a gnostic, a pantheist, a Swedenborgian, a Spinozan, a Manichee, a follower of Joachim of Fiore, a Platonist, or something else?[80] It can be added that Chesterton thought Blake had "a great deal of Swedenborg" and "a little of Cagliostro" (*Blake*, 125).

The point of ascertaining Blake's influences, though, is to reach a conclusion about his view of Christianity. Chesterton writes, "But in both cases [of Swedenborg and Cagliostro] it can be remarked that the mysticism marks an effort to escape from or even to forget the historic Christian, and especially the Catholic Church" (*Blake*, 124). Blake's religion

80. Davies, *The Theology of William Blake*, 2.

had little to do with the historical church. Like Watts, Blake's art often concerns primordial things and mythical stories. His pictures are charged with complex symbols and allegorical figures. Chesterton insists that Blake paints the *essence* of a thing; the first, primal fact is that a thing has an outline, a form, and a reality apart from our minds. In Chesterton's opinion, Blake's genius eclipses his digression and the irrelevance that was due to the esoteric fads of the eighteenth century. As Chesterton puts it, after we have allowed for such eccentricities due to the influence of Swedenborg and others, "All that follows is himself," that is, Blake the great creator and genius, whose theology took some unexpected turns, but is still in the end able to imagine so clearly those "eternal images of things," whether they are animals, people, or God himself, with unsurpassed power (*Blake*, 126, 160). Ultimately this is Blake's greatest triumph: the depiction of the Deity as the personal God who became incarnate. Other theologians have followed Chesterton in declaring that despite Blake's heterodoxy, the whole spirit of his art and poetry is undeniably Christian. At the very center of Blake's theology there is the joyous truth of personal God.[81]

From the beginning of his book Chesterton makes the case that Blake's belief in a personal, definite God is central to understanding all his literary and artistic work. On the first page Chesterton strikingly writes, "William Blake would have been the first to understand that the biography of anybody ought really to begin with the words, 'In the beginning God created heaven and earth. . . .' [T]he only right way of telling a story is to begin at the beginning—at the beginning of the world" (*Blake*, 1–2). William Blake's visual works express in a fantastic way the awesome imagination of the Divine itself. Despite his esoteric, spiritualist, and occult eccentricities, Blake's overall point of view was God-oriented and ultimately concerned with the knowability of God. Chesterton emphasizes this and thus describes him as having "a matured and massive supernaturalism" that is reflected in both style and content in his poems, artwork, and prophetic works (*Blake*, 9).

The essence of Blake's theology is found in his etchings for the Book of Job, and in numerous poems. Citing Blake's poem "Augeries of Innocence," Chesterton explicates Blake's theological genius (*Blake*, 147). The lines he has in mind are these:

> God appears, and God is light,
> To those poor souls who dwell in Night;

---

81. Davies, *The Theology of William Blake*, 161.

> But does a human form display
> To those who dwell in realms of Day.[82]

Blake says that God is blinding, impersonal light to those who dwell in night (that is, in ignorance), but to those who dwell in the day (that is, in imagination and wonder), God's true form is revealed as that of a man. The idea is echoed in Blake's seventeenth illustration for the Book of Job. The verse is Job 42:5, which reads, "I have heard thee with the hearing of the ear but now my eye seeth thee."[83] Blake provides a "final and fixed" image of this idea again; the sun pours out from a solid, muscular man, with a mighty beard that reaches nearly to the ground. This fixed figure is God himself. He is in the act of blessing Job and Job's wife as they face him. All the while, Job's friends are turned the other way, huddled together and cowering from this great God incarnate, this Ancient of Days (*Blake*, 44–45).

This figure of the Deity takes on a regular form in Blake's art. This is a Deity that is not an immaterial light nor an impersonal force; he is "the old man with the monstrous muscles, the mild stern eyebrows, the long smooth silver hair and beard" (*Blake*, 149). The idea is reflected in both Blake's poetry and his artwork. Urizen, a divine creator in Blake's mythical imagination, is likewise a concrete, personal being. In Blake's frontispiece for his *Europe: A Prophecy* he has depicted Urizen as the "Ancient of Days" in a scene of intense colors: he crouches in a posture of potential energy as he holds out a compass from the midst of elemental, blood-red clouds.[84] This shows that "God, though infinitely gigantic, should be as solid as a giant. . . . Here, according to his own conceptions, he may be said to have drawn God from the life" (*Blake*, 66). Whether or not Urizen is actually God is beside the point; Blake makes Urizen and his other divine characters correspond to God and the angels. These are personal, divine beings that are central to Blake's system. Chesterton enumerates the most important lessons of this universal artist when he writes on the final page, "[Blake] reiterates with passionate precision that which is lovable can be adorable, that deity is either a person or a puff of wind, that the more we know of higher things the more palpable and incarnate we shall find them; that the form filling the heavens is the likeness of the appearance of a man" (*Blake*, 210).

82. Sampson and Raleigh, *The Lyrical Poems of William Blake*, 142.
83. Damon, *Blake's Job*, 45.
84. Blake, *Europe: A Prophecy*, 17 plates relief etched.

Blake teaches us that all of creation is a wondrous outline of eternal realities and that God is more real, solid, and ultimately, incarnated, than any philosophers or Enlightenment freethinkers had ever guessed. In his insistence on these truths, communicated simultaneously through his art, poetry, and myth, Blake is a great genius—the "universalist" who achieves a balance of art and philosophy—who is able to outline eternity for us because God has given him, along with all of us, the divine power of creativity. This is the truth Chesterton finds in Blake's art; God has an outline—the outline of the incarnated Son of God, that is, Jesus Christ.

Conclusion

CHESTERTON'S THEOLOGICAL AESTHETIC

"For imagination is almost the opposite of illusion."[1]

G. K. CHESTERTON

IN THIS BOOK I have sketched the aesthetics of John Ruskin, Walter Pater, Oscar Wilde, and Gilbert Keith Chesterton. I have endeavored to demonstrate that in theoria, aesthesis, and symbolism, each writer makes *theological* claims. In considering their theologies I do not pretend that any of these men was a trained theologian. Instead, they were writers, novelists, teachers, and, most crucially for my argument, they were brilliant art and literary *critics* who did not simply accept the religious fragmentation of their age but offered interpretations of beauty that could lead their readers or disciples to a religious return. In the case of Ruskin, this return comes through the contemplative practice of theoria, which stems from Ruskin's early Evangelical beliefs. With Pater and Wilde, the pathway to a kind of religion is through the charm of art itself, a charm that took on religious dimensions, but with Wilde at least, did lead to an actual conversion to Roman Catholicism. Finally, in Chesterton's aesthetics and art criticism there is a recovery of Christianity, a symbolist reappraisal of imagination and creativity in the artist that led Chesterton to insist that each artist repeats in the microcosm of the canvas what God does in the macrocosm

1. Chesterton, *Autobiography*, 31.

of creation. Let me briefly revisit each critic's particular approach before offering final comments on Chesterton's theological aesthetic.

John Ruskin sees the natural world as the mode of God's revelation that complements the revelation of the Bible. Ruskin's Evangelicalism and Victorian "honest doubt" contribute to an aesthetic that seeks to cope with the loss-of-faith narrative that scholars such as Miller, Shaffer, and others have elucidated. The aesthetic contemplative faculty, theoria, inhabits the realm of natural theology. Ruskin's characterization of God in his monumental *Modern Painters* is that of a magnanimous Father figure, speaking gracious words to humanity and bestowing lavish gifts upon them. From the right knowledge or spiritual perception of these gifts, people are able to know God in some way. Artists, especially landscape artists, thus have the duty to tell this truth of God to the populace. Art is a deeply moral endeavor because, like any other activity, it is either rooted in one's faith in God and moral duty to humanity or it flows from one's own selfishness, pride, and doubt and leads to blasphemy, error, and lies. To fully establish this connection between beauty, morality, truth, and God, Ruskin establishes the most important theological aesthetic in England during the nineteenth century, an aesthetic he explains in the many brilliant passages of *Modern Painters I* and *II*. However, as I argue in chapter 1, Ruskin is unable to account for imperfection, sin, or suffering in his system. Ruskin did indeed have a rich and complicated relationship to the established church, and he went through an intense period of searching and doubt in the middle of his life. Those facts are not in question here, but rather, what is in question is the place Ruskin's theoria has for Christ as the revealed God *in human flesh*. The answer, as we have seen, is nowhere. In *Modern Painters II* we see Ruskin's disgust with the crucifixion scenes painted by Giotto and Fra Angelico. We read of his distrust of "Romanism" trying to "excite the languid sympathies of its untaught flocks" through the images of Christ bleeding and of Christ suffering (MP II, 201). We encounter his views of ancient Greek art compared to mediaeval Italian art; Greek art (and neo-classical art) with its fleshy, muscular forms are far from the truth of actual bodies and are aberrations. Ruskin writes, "No herculean form is spiritual, for it is degrading the spiritual creature to suppose it operative through impulse of bone and sinew; its power is immaterial and constant . . ." (MP II, 327). This is crucial to our understanding of theoria.

In this critical age of "honest doubt," Walter Pater finds newfound meaning and great glory in the human body, with its skin, muscles, and bones. In one of Pater's essays on the artist-poet Dante Gabriel Rossetti, he writes, "Practically, the church of the Middle Age by its aesthetic worship, its sacramentalism, its real faith in the resurrection of the flesh, had set itself up against the Manichean opposition of spirit and matter, and its results in men's way of taking life."[2] Pater goes on to say, "Dante is the central representative of its spirit. To him, in the vehement and impassioned heat of his conceptions, the material and the spiritual are fused and blend: if the spiritual attains the definite visibility of a crystal, what is material loses its earthiness and impurity."[3] Pater's problem is that his "art for art's sake" may approach the outer forms of this medieval sacramentalism he appreciated, but it cannot achieve anything beyond the luster and glow of the matter itself. For him life is a series of gasps until one finally dies. To burn with great passion should be the final goal of each person.

Pater understands better than most art critics of his time the inextricable union of flesh and spirit in Catholic Christianity. He identifies and lambasts the prudish distaste of the flesh that he saw all around him in the Christendom of the Victorian Age. So, he reacts. He rejects these and all other dogmas; he will have only feelings, only sensations. These are so brilliant, so shimmering, that they have the power of liberating a person from her or his situation, and can open up a "new kingdom of feeling, and sensation, and thought, not opposed to but only beyond and independent of the spiritual system . . ." (*Renaissance*, 6). While Pater does not unveil God in human flesh, that is, the Christ, he does suggest in his writings a longing for a kind of sacramental encounter, an experience that would govern one's whole life by its power and complexity: "Not the fruit of experience, but experience itself, is the end" (*Renaissance*, 236). There is a beautiful sacramentality expressed here; it is a desire not for the benefits of an experience, but for the very experience itself. The experience, or the union, the encounter—this, and not its perks, is what Pater suggests we must strive for.

Yet Pater's conclusion in *The Renaissance* is that a real relationship with the Divine is unattainable; instead, all that can be done is to desperately grasp for truth, meaning, and God in a world of where things have no meaning above their own immanent charm. For no amount of exquisite experiences can, apart from a telos, lead to the "breaking of the

2. Warner and Hough, *Strangeness and Beauty*, 2:67.

3. Warner and Hough, *Strangeness and Beauty*, 2:67–68.

light."[4] No amount of exquisite, "vital forces" can stave off death. Pater's final command to the reader (i.e., the critic) is to "see and touch," and to do this so often that there is not time to even concoct theories. But this is a contradiction itself, for Pater's conclusion constitutes a theory—a theory of "art for art's sake." This aesthesis in Pater provides a framework for interpreting sensual perceptions, but not for organizing them, making sense of them, or directing them. Pater's disciple, Oscar Wilde, would take his "art for art's sake" credo a step further.

For Wilde, aesthetic contemplation should be the goal and end of every person's life. For beauty is the "symbol of symbols. . . . When it shows itself, it shows us the whole fiery-coloured world" (*Intentions*, 158). Beauty is revelatory and transformative; it constitutes "real life." The workaday world must not change or sully our perception of beauty. Wilde writes that "it is none the less true that Life imitates Art far more than Art imitates Life" (*Intentions*, 90). Ruskin would disagree, while Chesterton would agree with a qualification. It is true, Wilde might remind us, that the Greeks would place a beautiful statue near the bridal bed, under the assumption that beauty in the heart gives birth to beauty in life and in the body (*Intentions*, 91). During his time, Wilde realized that artists must not attempt to use beauty as a tool for some other purpose, because when ethics and art are mingled, art becomes impure, corrupted. Indeed, Wilde sensed that the power of beauty was lessened when it was harnessed to some other purpose than the mere purpose of creating exquisite delight, in short, a mood (*Intentions*, 179). In insisting on the separation of aesthetics from any metaphysical or religious system, Wilde critiques Ruskin's theoria, with its tendency to devalue the flesh in all its physicality, but Wilde offers no alternative direction, no means to fully realize where beauty might actually take humanity. The critic is a person with the gift of sifting experiences and pulling out those that delight the most. It is criticism, so Wilde believes, that will lead to progress for humanity. Criticism will eliminate "race-prejudices by insisting upon the unity of the human mind in the variety of its forms" (*Intentions*, 203); indeed, critics will eventually carry Europe to "the perfection of which the saints have dreamed" (*Intentions*, 205). But in this picture Wilde has no real answers as to why eliminating "race-prejudices" is good, or why saintly perfection is desirable. With no God in his aesthesis, Wilde's

4. Pater writes, "He who is ever looking for the breaking of a light he knows not whence about him, notes with a strange heedfulness the faintest paleness in the sky," quoted in Warner and Hough, *Strangeness and Beauty*, 2:11.

Intentions themselves become beautiful lies. His very criticism is a work of art that delights and provokes without giving a substantial answer to the fragmentation of the age and the quest for what many Victorians saw as a disappearing God.

Then G. K. Chesterton arose in 1899–1900. He may seem to be an unlikely figure to pull together these different aesthetic approaches, yet he does just this, and in his art criticism he makes an original contribution that has been for the most part ignored. A brilliant stylist and humorist, Chesterton came onto the literary scene in an abrupt and unexpected way, first by writing reviews of art books for *The Bookman* and other short review pieces for the *Daily News*. With his *G. F. Watts* (1904) and later his *William Blake* (1910), Chesterton articulates a theological aesthetic that directly encounters theoria and aesthesis at the close of the century. Chesterton's aesthetic is a symbolist response to the doubt and skepticism of the age, rooted in the Christian conception of Jesus Christ as the Son of Man and Son of God, incarnated for humanity's sake. All symbols, beautiful and even ugly, reflect in some way the fundamental truths of humanity, made in the image of God and saved by the Image of God (Christ). Spirit and flesh are combined in what is the greatest symbol and paradox: the incarnation.

I have demonstrated why I interpret his position in view of the symbolist movement, and why I see it as something that pulls a variety of approaches together, that is, it combines Ruskin's theological center with Pater and Wilde's attention to the human body. Perhaps, more deeply, Chesterton embraces Ruskin's turn to God with Pater and Wilde's emphasis on the priestly functions of both the artist and the critic. Chesterton does not think that the artist must have fidelity to the outward vision of nature, but to the inward vision of man/woman. It has been given to all people to become artists, that is, to *draw* the truth out of things. The style of art does not always matter, but only whether the style expresses each human's divinely gifted imagination and creative power. Without arguing about the existence of God, Chesterton sees that the image of God in woman and in man is an amazing, recognizable fact of our existence. Each individual is capable of being an artist with divine powers, divine vision, and divine creativity. Each individual is able to unveil and reveal the eternal, mysterious things of God. This is the power of art, and art is found in virtually every human endeavor. So for Chesterton, everything from landscape paintings to portraits to caricatures and puppets can perform this revelatory power.

In arguing all of this, I hopefully have also demonstrated that Chesterton deserves to be seen as a noteworthy art critic in his own right. Because of his vast journalistic output and his autodidacticism, which confounds any scholarly enquiry into discovering the sources of many of his views, parsing out particular theories from Chesterton may be a difficult task. This is why his *Autobiography*, in which he outlines his many friendships and influences, is such an aid.

In reflecting on his life, Chesterton reflects on the place of imagination in his childhood, and he writes about his earliest memory, one that had a significant impact on his entire development and spirituality; it is a scene he witnessed as a little child. The second chapter begins as follows:

> The very first thing I can ever remember seeing with my own eyes was a young man walking across a bridge. He had a curly moustache and an attitude of confidence verging on swagger. He carried in his hand a disproportionately large key of a shining yellow metal and wore a large golden or gilded crown. . . . In the castle there was one window, out of which a young lady was looking.[5]

These reflections shed light upon his entire body of work, and they are immensely entertaining because Chesterton does not preface them with any information about the fictional or nonfictional status of the setting, objects, and characters. This is a puppet show he is describing, and it is the most powerful *symbol* of his life. Reaching beyond any fictional/nonfictional or temporal/eternal divide, it is rather apocalyptic: an unveiling of deeper, eternal realities in the present (which Chesterton can continually relive). He writes that this particular scene "glows in my memory like a glimpse of some incredible paradise."[6] For him it comes to represent the idea that most people have forgotten the divine truth, the magic, that penetrates all of reality. It is through the romantic thrill of the toy theatre that we remember that we have forgotten something, that we have been looking at life wrongly.

The puppets are symbols for Chesterton, but of exactly what he does not reveal until the final chapter of the book. Here he reminisces about a trip he once took. He was walking with a friend in a Polish town when the friend said, "You take off your hat here." Chesterton obliged, without knowing why, and then tells the reader,

5. Chesterton, *Autobiography*, 31.

6. Chesterton, *Autobiography*, 34.

> And then I saw the open street. It was filled with a vast crowd,
> all facing me; and all on their knees on the ground. It was as if
> someone were walking behind me; or some strange bird were
> hovering over my head. I faced round, and saw in the centre
> of the arch great windows standing open, unsealing a chamber
> full of gold and colours; there was a picture behind; but parts
> of the whole picture were moving like a puppet-show, stirring
> strange double memories like a dream of the bridge in the
> puppet-show of my childhood; and then I realised that from
> those shifting groups there shone and sounded the ancient
> magnificence of the Mass.[7]

The puppet show symbolizes the magic that the Mass enacts, where the priest reveals the great truth, Christ himself, through ordinary means. There the full, sacramental presence of Christ's body and blood are soon to be found in the common, earthly elements. Only one must have the eyes of faith to see such an unveiling. One must have eyes like Chesterton's to see that the world and all the things in it are truly astonishing because they are true symbols, participating with the eternal. One must have eyes of faith, wonder, and gratitude to see one's own unique self, made in the image of God and gifted with creative powers—such powers that allow others to see the greatness of the gift and therefore of the Giver. Each artist is a divine symbol, that is, he or she symbolizes the divine creativity of God, his wondrous imagination and fathomless love. If we perceive God in the natural world, then we also must perceive him in one another, tiny creators that we are. God gives us colors and canvasses and all the rest to make little worlds: paintings and toys and puppets because we are his children, and all material things are imbued with Divine presence, capable of demonstrating God, sharing God, and honoring God. Many of us have been looking falsely at material things, such as art or the theater or the Mass; perhaps, our lives would be very different if we could look at them with the gratitude and wonder of G. K. Chesterton.

7. Chesterton, *Autobiography*, 318.

Bibliography

Arnold, Matthew. "Dover Beach." In *The Poetical Works of Matthew Arnold*, edited by C. B. Tinker and H. F. Lowry, 210–12. London: Oxford University Press, 1950.

———. *Literature & Dogma: An Essay Towards a Better Apprehension of the Bible*. London: Watts, 1910.

Bal, Mieke. *Reading Rembrandt: Beyond the Word-Image Opposition*. Cambridge: Cambridge University Press, 1991.

Barfield, Owen. *What Coleridge Thought*. London: Oxford University Press, 1971.

Beaumont, Matthew, and Matthew Ingleby. *G. K. Chesterton, London and Modernity*. London: Bloomsbury Academic, 2013.

Beaumont, Sheona, and Madeleine Emerald Thiele, eds. *John Ruskin, the Pre-Raphaelites, and Religious Imagination*. London: Palgrave Macmillan, 2023.

Bills, Mark, and Barbara Bryant. *G. F. Watts: Victorian Visionary: Highlights from the Watts Gallery Collection*. New Haven, CT: Yale University Press, 2008.

Birch, Dinah. *Ruskin's Myths*. Oxford: Oxford University Press, 1988.

Blake, William. *Europe: A Prophecy*. Seventeen plates relief etched, Lambeth, Special Collection RX 132, Glasgow University Library, Special Collections Department, 1794.

———. *William Blake: The Complete Illuminated Books*. London: Thames and Hudson, 2001.

Canovan, Margaret. *G. K. Chesterton: Radical Populist*. New York: Harcourt Brace Jovanovich, 1977.

Chesterton, G. K. *Autobiography*. London: Hutchinson, 1936.

———. *The Colored Lands*. Mineola, NY: Dover, 2009.

———. *The Everlasting Man*. San Francisco: Ignatius, 2008.

———. "Famous Novelists in the National Portrait Gallery." *The Bookman* 21[123] (1901) n.p.

———. *G. F. Watts*. London: Duckworth, 1904.

———. *A Handful of Authors*. London: Sheed and Ward, 1953.

———. *Heretics*. London: John Lane: The Bodley Head, 1919.

———. "The Literary Portraits of G. F. Watts, R.A." *The Bookman* 19.111 (December 1900) 80–83.

———. *Magic: A Fantastic Comedy*. London: Martin Secker & Warburg, 1936.

———. *Orthodoxy*. London: John Lane: The Bodley Head, 1927.

———. "Ruskin." *The Speaker: The Liberal Review* 2 (1900) 107–8.

———. "The Ruskin Reader." *The Academy* 47.1206 (1895) 523.

————. *St. Thomas Aquinas—St. Francis of Assisi, in One Volume.* San Francisco: Ignatius, 1986.

————. *Tremendous Trifles.* New York: Dood, Mead, 1929.

————. *Varied Types.* London: A. L. Humphreys, 1902.

————. *William Blake.* London: Duckworth, 1910.

Chesterton, G. K., with J. E. Hodder Williams. "Literary Pictures of the Year." *The Bookman* 18.105 (June 1900) 79–84.

————. "Literary Pictures of the Year: II—The Three Classes of Literary Art." *The Bookman* 18.106 (July 1900) 112–16.

————. "Literary Pictures of the Year: II—The Three Classes of Literary Art—(Continued)." *The Bookman* 18.107 (August 1900) 141–42.

————. *Thomas Carlyle, with Numerous Illustrations.* London: Hodder and Stoughton, 1902.

Coleridge, Samuel Taylor. *Biographia Literaria.* London: Dent, 1947.

Collingwood, R. G. *Ruskin's Philosophy.* Kendal, UK: Wilson, 1922.

Collingwood, W. G., ed. *The Ruskin Reader.* London: George Allen, 1895.

Conlon, D. J. *G. K. Chesterton: A Half Century of Views.* Oxford: Oxford University Press, 1987.

————. *G. K. Chesterton: A Reappraisal.* York, UK: Methuen, 2015.

Cook, E. T., and Alexander Wedderburn, eds. *The Works of John Ruskin.* Vol. 3. London: George Allen, 1903.

————. *The Works of John Ruskin.* Vol. 4. London: George Allen, 1904.

————. *The Works of John Ruskin.* Vol. 29. London: George Allen, 1907.

Chipp, Herschel B., ed. *Theories of Modern Art: A Source Book by Artists and Critics.* London: University of California Press, 1968.

Dale, Alzina Stone. *The Art of G. K. Chesterton.* Chicago: Loyola University Press, 1985.

Damon, S. Foster. *Blake's Job: William Blake's Illustrations of the Book of Job.* Providence, RI: Brown University Press, 1966.

Danson, Lawrence. *Wilde's Intentions: The Artist in His Criticism.* Oxford: Clarendon, 1997.

Davies, J. G. *The Theology of William Blake.* Oxford: Clarendon, 1948.

Drabble, Margaret, ed. *The Oxford Companion to English Literature.* Oxford: Oxford University Press, 1985.

Edwards, L. Clifton. *Creation's Beauty as Revelation: Toward a Creational Theology of Natural Beauty.* Eugene, OR: Pickwick, 2014.

Ellmann, Richard. *Oscar Wilde.* London: Hamish Hamilton, 1987.

Everett Gilbert, Katharine, and Helmut Kuhn. *A History of Esthetics.* New York: Macmillan, 1939.

Fagerberg, David. *The Size of Chesterton's Catholicism.* Notre Dame, IN: University of Notre Dame Press, 1998.

Fraser, Hilary. *Beauty and Belief: Aesthetics and Religion in Victorian Literature.* Cambridge: Cambridge University Press, 1986.

Fuller, Peter. *Theoria: Art, and the Absence of Grace.* London: Chatto & Windus, 1988.

Guy, Josephine ed. *The Complete Works of Oscar Wilde.* Vol. 4, *Criticism: Historical Criticism, Intentions, The Soul of Man.* Oxford: Oxford University Press, 2007.

Guyer, Paul. *A History of Modern Aesthetics.* Vol. 2, *The Nineteenth Century.* New York: Cambridge University Press, 2014.

Herbert, Robert L. *The Art Criticism of John Ruskin.* Garden City, NY: Anchor, 1964.

Hext, Kate. *Walter Pater: Individualism and Aesthetic Philosophy*. Edinburgh: Edinburgh University Press, 2013.

Hilton, Tim. *John Ruskin*. New Haven, CT: Yale University Press, 2002.

Juurikkala, Oskari. "The Two Books of God: The Metaphor of the Book of Nature in Augustine." *Augustinianum* 61.2 (2021) 479–98.

Ker, Ian. *G. K. Chesterton*. London: Oxford University Press, 2012.

Knight, Mark, and Emma Mason. *Nineteenth-Century Religion and Literature: An Introduction*. Oxford: Oxford University Press, 2006.

Landow, George P. *The Aesthetic and Critical Theories of John Ruskin*. Princeton: Princeton University Press, 1971.

———. *Victorian Types, Victorian Shadows: Biblical Typology in Victorian Literature, Art and Thought*. London: Routledge & Kegan Paul, 1980.

Larrissy, Edward, ed. *W. B. Yeats*. Oxford: Oxford University Press, 1997.

Larsen, Timothy. *Crisis of Doubt: Honest Faith in 19th Century England*. Oxford: Oxford University Press, 2006.

Lauer, Quentin. *G. K. Chesterton: Philosopher without Portfolio*. New York: Fordham University Press, 2004.

Merrill, Linda. *A Pot of Paint: Aesthetics on Trial in Whistler v. Ruskin*. Washington, DC: Smithsonian. 1993.

Merton, Thomas. *Contemplative Prayer*. New York: Image Doubleday, 1996.

Milbank, Allison. *Chesterton and Tolkien as Theologians: The Fantasy of the Real*. London: T. & T. Clark, 2009.

Miller, J. Hillis. *The Disappearance of God: Five Nineteenth-Century Writers*. Cambridge, MA: Harvard University Press, 1963.

Murdoch, Iris. *The Fire & The Sun: Why Plato Banished the Artists*. Based upon the Romanes Lecture 1976. Oxford: Clarendon, 1977.

Nichols, Aidan. *All Great Art Is Praise: Art and Religion in John Ruskin*. Washington, DC: Catholic University of American Press, 2017.

Oddie, William. *Chesterton and the Romance of Orthodoxy: The Making of GKC 1874–1908*. Oxford: Oxford University Press, 2008.

O'Hear, Anthony. *Transcendence, Creation, and Incarnation: From Philosophy to Religion*. London: Routledge, 2020.

Osborn, Eric. *Tertullian: First Theologian of the West*. Cambridge: Cambridge University Press, 1997.

Parker, James. "A Most Unlikely Saint." *The Atlantic* [online], April 2017. https://www.theatlantic.com/magazine/archive/2015/04/a-most-unlikely-saint/386243/.

Pater, Walter. *Marius the Epicurean*. 2 vols. London: MacMillan, 1885.

———. *The Renaissance: Studies in Art and Poetry*. Reprint, Chicago: Pandora Academy, 1978.

Pattison, George. *Art, Modernity, and Faith*. London: SCM, 1998.

Peters, Thomas C. *The Christian Imagination: G. K. Chesterton on the Arts*. San Francisco: Ignatius, 2000.

Renan, Ernest. *The Life of Jesus. Complete Edition*. London: Watts, 1935.

Reyburn, Duncan. *Seeing Things as They Are: G. K. Chesterton and the Drama of Meaning*. Veritas. Eugene, OR: Cascade, 2016.

Reynolds, Joshua. *Fifteen Discourses Delivered in the Royal Academy*. London: Dent, 1928.

Ruskin, John. *The Bible References in the Works of John Ruskin*. Arranged by Mary and Ellen Gibbs. London: George Allen, 1898.

Sampson, John, and Walter Raleigh, eds. *The Lyrical Poems of William Blake*. Oxford: Oxford University Press, 1905.

Schindler, D. C. *Plato's Critique of Impure Reason: On Goodness and Truth in the Republic*. Washington, DC: Catholic University of America Press, 2008.

Shaffer, E. S. *"Kubla Khan" and the Fall of Jerusalem: The Mythological School in Biblical Criticism and Secular Literature, 1770–1880*. London: Cambridge University Press, 1975.

Simpson, David, ed. *German Aesthetic and Literary Criticism: Kant, Fichte, Schelling, Schopenhauer, Hegel*. Cambridge: Cambridge University Press, 1984.

Stapleton, Julia, ed. *G. K. Chesterton at the Daily News*. Part 1, vol. 1, *Literature, Liberalism and Revolution, 1901–1913*. London: Routledge, 2012.

Stokstad, Marilyn, and David Cateforis. *Art History*. 2nd ed. Upper Saddle River, NJ: Pearson/ Prentice Hall, 2005.

Strauss, David. *The Life of Jesus Critically Examined*. 4th ed. Translated by George Eliot. London: Swan Sonnenschein, 1902.

Symons, Arthur. *The Symbolist Movement in Literature*. Manchester: Carcanet, 2014.

Trodd, Colin, and Stephanie Brown, eds. *Representations of G. F. Watts*. Farmham, UK: Ashgate, 2004.

Underhill, Evelyn. *Mysticism: A Study in the Nature and Development of Man's Spiritual Consciousness*. New York: Dutton, 1961.

Unterecker, John. *A Reader's Guide to William Butler Yeats*. New York: Noonday, 1959.

Van Horn, Michael A. *Within My Heart: The Enlightenment Epistemic Reversal and the Subjective Justification of Religious Belief*. Eugene, OR: Pickwick, 2017.

Von Hügel, Friedrich. *The Mystical Element of Religion as Studied in Saint Catherine of Genoa and Her Friends*. New York: Crossroad, 1999.

Warner, Eric, and Graham Hough, eds. *Strangeness and Beauty: An Anthology of Aesthetic Criticism, 1840–1910*. Vol. 1, *Ruskin to Swinburne*. Cambridge: Cambridge University Press, 1983.

———. *Strangeness and Beauty: An Anthology of Aesthetic Criticism, 1840–910*. Vol. 2, *Pater to Arthur Symons*. Cambridge: Cambridge University Press, 1983.

Wheeler, Michael. *Ruskin's God*. Cambridge: Cambridge University Press, 1999.

White, R. J., ed. *Political Tracts of Wordsworth, Coleridge, and Shelley*. Cambridge: Cambridge University Press, 1953.

Whiteley, Giles. *Aestheticism and the Philosophy of Death: Walter Pater and Post-Hegelianism*. London: Legenda, 2010.

Wild, Robert. *The Tumbler of God: Chesterton as Mystic*. Tacoma, WA: Angelico, 2013.

Wills, Gary. *Chesterton*. New York: Image Doubleday, 2001.

Name Index